MISSION

MISSION

An
ESSENTIAL GUIDE

Carlos F. Cardoza-Orlandi

Abingdon Press
Nashville

MISSION
AN ESSENTIAL GUIDE

Copyright © 2002 by Abingdon Press

This book is printed on recycled, acid-free, elemental-chlorine–free paper.

Library of Congress Cataloging-in-Publication Data

Orlandi, Carlos F. Cardoza, 1961-
  Mission : an essential guide / Carlos F. Cardoza Orlandi.
    p. cm.
Includes bibliographical references.
  ISBN 0-687-05472-9 (pbk. : alk. paper)
  1. Missions—Theory. I. Title.
  BV2063 .075 2002
  266—dc21

2001008439

All scripture quotations are from the *New Revised Standard Version of the Bible,* copyright 1989, by the Division of Christian Education of the National Council of the Churches of Christ in the United States of America. Used by permission. All rights reserved.

Excerpt from *Teaching Mission in a Global Context* copyright © 2001 by Patricia Lloyd-Sidle. Used by permission of Westminster John Knox Press.

Excerpt from "En medio de la vida" copyright © 1979 by Mortimer Arias. Used by permission.

02 03 04 05 06 07 08 09 10 11—10 9 8 7 6 5 4 3 2 1

MANUFACTURED IN THE UNITED STATES OF AMERICA

To the Hispanic/Latino communities in the United States,
teachers of intercultural mission;

To the Iglesia Evangélica Española (Spanish Evangelical Church)
in the Bronx;

To Sinaí Christian Church (Disciples of Christ) in Brooklyn;

To the Tercera Iglesia Cristiana (Third Hispanic Church,
Discípulos de Cristo) on the west side;

And to La Hermosa Christian Church (Disciples of Christ)
in Manhattan

Acknowledgment

I would like to express my gratitude to Columbia Theological Seminary and the Lilly 2000–2001 Faculty Grant of the Association of Theological Schools for their support during the concluding phase of this Essential Guide.

Contents

Objects and Subjects of Mission

A New Perspective

I am excited about the future of Christian mission! Christian communities seek ways to be faithful to the gospel of Jesus Christ, and in their search they have discovered God's missionary work among them, beyond them, and at times, despite them! In this search, Christian communities struggle to discern their missionary calling, sending, and doing. They read Scriptures, study history, reflect theologically, and develop programs, which they hope will be congruent with their understanding of missionary activity. Significant numbers of congregations have not given up on their call to be "missionary people."

Nevertheless, many congregations, and particularly many mainstream Protestant congregations, find themselves at odds in this process of discernment. Their mission history—congregational and denominational—their theologies, their practices of ministry, and their traditional missionary programs fall short of providing adequate tools to understand the context and the incarnation of the gospel in today's complex contexts. Pastors, lay leaders, mission leaders, and students of mission are seeking resources that will help them move beyond mission theologies and practices considered outdated and unacceptable in this day. We need a refreshing perspective to read the times, to discern our calling, and to act, as missiologist David Bosch said, "with bold humility" in the name of God.

Mission: An Essential Guide is written with a particular perspective that may help the reader rethink and rediscover mission in a new way—a perspective from one who was missionized and who believes in mission. Most mission textbooks in English are written by writers from the Euro-Atlantic context who have missionary experience and who have a deep commitment to the gospel. There are a few written by writers in the Southern continents,[1] but most of these focus on one dimension of missionary work—interreligious dialogue, contextualization, interpretation of Scripture, and so forth. Very few English texts, whose purpose is to provide a general but informed perspective on mission, are written from the side of those who experience a double identity: we have been the *object of mission* and we are *subjects of mission*.

This book presents a missional reflection from a Caribbean/Hispanic-Latino perspective. This means that in a very particular way, I share my missional knowledge and perspective from the experience of being missionized. At times, being the *object of mission* symbolized a religious and social location that assumed that my cultures were inferior and that my multiple religious backgrounds were deficient. As one who has been missionized, one who has been the *object of mission*, I am expected to be grateful for the gospel transmitted, civilized by the education given, and bold for the cause of the Reign of God. Regrettably, I was not expected to be critical of the methods and practices used to transmit the gospel, assertive and inquisitive of my own diverse cultural background, and determined to understand the meaning and cause of God's Reign in a different context. In other words, I was never expected to become a *subject of mission*.

As I become aware of my dual communal identity in a Christian community—as the *object and subject of mission*—I find no harm in exploring, studying, and critically reflecting on the mission theologies and practices that I have inherited. I find no harm in disregarding theologies and practices of mission that did not fully embody the gospel. I find no harm in finding myself in a paradox as I try to rethink mission theologies and practices that need to combine the old and the new. I find no harm, but rather an invitation from the Holy Spirit to seek for mission theologies and practices that can proclaim, in word and deed, the fullness of the gospel of the Reign of God. In other words, I find myself in an exciting paradox, between *discontinuity and continuity*, as I seek for tools that will help Christian communities be in mission without losing the awareness that we are both *objects and subjects of mission*. It is this dual identity as God's missionary people, identity that will be discussed throughout this book, that gives *Mission: An Essential Guide* a humble and new perspective for developing theologies and practices of mission.

From *Missions* to *Mission* to *Missiology*

"The church exists by mission, just as fire exists by burning." With these words, theologian Emil Brunner described the importance of mission for the life of the church of Jesus Christ. Christians define their identity through their mission work, the clear and effective communication of the gospel of Christ. To be the church is to be in mission.

Traditionally, the term "mission" has been confused with the term "missions." For many Christians, "missions" refers to the activities that the church does to communicate the gospel to those who are non-Christian. Therefore, it is very common to find the term "missions" conveying overseas ministry, a crossing of geographical boundaries, and/or a ministry beyond the national church or denomination. The understanding has been that the church does "missions" when it sends missionaries to foreign countries.

That definition of "missions" is limiting for several important reasons. First, "missions" is understood to be the activity of the church or ecclesiastical group. This understanding means that the focus of the missionary activity is the institution, such as the church, the denomination, or the missionary organization. The institution, then, as the recipient of salvation, initiates, develops, and finishes the task to be done. The second limitation is the understanding that "missions" is directed toward non-Christians. Non-Christians are not part of the church; hence, they are unsaved. The assumption is often that God has not been part of their lives because *the church* has not been part of their lives. Cyprian's classic statement *salus extra ecclesiam non est* (E. 73.21), "salvation outside the church does not exist," often informs "missions." Therefore, the goal of missionary activity becomes making non-Christians members of a church.

This understanding of "missions" presents some biblical and theological problems. For example, the concept of "missions" has the church, denomination, or missionary organization as its principal protagonist. However, the Bible testifies that the protagonist of all missionary activity is God. John 17:18 and 20:21 are clear examples of the centrality of God in missionary activity. These texts also illustrate the relationship that exists between the act of God sending the Son, and the act of the Son sending the disciples.

The relationship between the senders (God and the Son), those who are sent (the Son and the disciples), and the world dissipates in the understanding of "missions." A Christian focus on the church's missionary activity tends to forget that missionary activity begins in and with God, and that such activity has a relational character between the One who sends, those who are sent, and the world. In other words, all missionary activity points beyond itself to bear witness to what God is doing in the world and to the new relationship this witness creates between God and creation. The church is not the sender but the one that is sent.

In summary, on the one hand, the concept of "missions" is often permeated by a history of a religious messianism, in which the church has understood itself to be the only responsible party for the witness of the gospel. On the other hand, the objects of the gospel have often been seen exclusively as non-Christians, unsaved people. Frequently and mistakenly, no other concept or practice of mission seems to exist outside these two camps.

In many congregations, this understanding of "missions" is disguised with medical, educational, and housing projects. At the forefront, "missions" becomes an activity that congregations support in order to help the disadvantaged rise above their poverty and obtain adequate living conditions. However, behind these activities, there is the assumption and expectation that those who are unsaved will be aware of God's love for them and will convert from their "heathenism." Moreover, there is an increasing interest in congregations about mission that still carries "missions" understandings.

Correctly understood, the term "mission," and particularly the mission of the church, broadens the understanding and practice of "missions." For example, "mission" does not exclude the evangelization of non-Christians, but it does include the recognition that God initiates all missionary activity, and that God, as a missionary God, participates with those whom God sends. In this missionary activity, God and those who are sent relate to the world. Since God is in mission, the church is missionary. In other words, the mission of God is the mission of the church, and those who are sent on such a mission are in an intense relationship with both God and the world. There is no mission apart from God, and there is no church without mission. Hence, we can talk about the mission of the church because God is in mission and because we profess a missionary God. Mission is a spiritual discipline, informed by prayer, devotion, communal worship, biblical study, and critical theological reflection. *Mission is the participation of the people of God in God's action in the world.* The theological and critical reflection about mission is called *missiology.* This book introduces the reader to some aspects of missiology.

Outline of the Book

The first chapter of this guide offers an important theological lesson from missiology. Any reflection about mission needs to be *contextualized.* This means that we need to take seriously the cultural, economic, social, political, and religious situation of the place from where mission originates. Those who have been missionized, who are partners in mission, often provide a critical assessment of the missionaries' understanding of the gospel and their practice of mission. Consequently, those partners become "mirrors" who reflect our mission theologies and practices, hence providing a critical evaluation of mission practice and an opportunity for change and renewal. As a partner in mission, in this chapter I explore the *captivity of mission models.* These models help the reader both map out the practice of mission in many congregations in the North American context and understand how cross-cultural missiology can serve as a liberating force for congregations.

The second chapter proposes a definition of mission. By integrating biblical, theological, and missiological studies, it explores the significance of mission as the action of God and the dilemmas and challenges that confront the people of God as we participate in God's missionary activity.

The third chapter expounds upon the contemporary missiological and biblical discussions about the church's mission. The Holy Scriptures offer Christians invaluable guidance for the mission of the church of Jesus Christ. No longer is "The Great Commission" (Matthew 28:16-20) the only text on which to reflect on the mission and participation of the people of God in the world. Biblical scholars, exegetes, and missiologists are discovering multiple perspectives that nourish, revise, and renew our understanding about the nature of mission.

The fourth chapter presents, first of all, the most common theologies of mission discussed today. Most of these theologies hold a strong missiological reflection of the West, particularly Western Europe and the United States, though most of them emerged as the result of intercultural and interreligious encounters in mission history. They represent, in distinct historical moments, strong debates and divisions among missiologists and missionary organizations.

Second, these theologies also represent the increasing contribution of the global Christian communities, particularly from the Southern/Eastern regions, to missiological thought and practice. These missiological models emerge from the experience and reflection of the people of God in every corner of the world, thus reflecting the global and ecumenical nature of the church's mission. Moreover, these theologies, ecumenical in nature, represent the broad spectrum of missiological thought and practice in most Roman Catholic, Evangelical, Pentecostal, and Orthodox circles around the world. This chapter, therefore, serves as a prism of critical reflection of the people of God as they participate in God's mission.

The fifth chapter helps local congregations consider their role in mission. This chapter helps leaders reflect on the church's mission, intercultural encounters, the sacramental nature of mission, evangelization, and justice. It also provides some strategies for short mission trips, long-term mission involvement, and ecumenical and interfaith ministries.

The sixth chapter provides the reader with some ideas about theological or Christian education and mission. Many congregations are looking for ways in which a mission education program can be part of the Christian education ministry. This chapter suggests themes and disciplines that may be included if such a program is to be implemented in a congregation or a community.

The conclusion discusses both the nature and process of practices and theologies of mission. I also included my own faith-in-mission statement, giving witness to the spiritual character of reflecting on mission theologies and practices. The faith-in-mission statement is also an invitation for the reader to discover and reflect on her or his own practice and theology of mission as part of a Christian community.

Finally, the book concludes with a bibliography for further reading and a glossary.

Let us begin our missiological journey and conversation.

---

1. The term *Southern continents* refers to the Two-Thirds world, Third World countries, or developing nations.

CHAPTER ONE

The Captivity of Mission in North American Churches

Mission is a term of multiple and intense meanings. On the one hand, it evokes responsibility, outreach, overseas service, funds, cooperation, unity, redemption, conversion, dialogue, witness, and so forth. On the other hand, it brings to mind such negative elements as colonialism, cultural and religious superiority, imposition of denominations, dependency, and exploitation. Historically, mission reminds the church of both its benevolent intentions with disastrous results, and its cruel actions with redeeming effects. Psychologically, reactions to mission swing from rejection and indifference, to passionate and enthusiastic engagement.

In many ways, mission simultaneously embodies the grace of God and the evil of human arrogance and worldly interests. Mission entails ambiguity and the risk of walking the narrow path with big stumbling feet! From a Four-Fifths World perspective—the perspective of the Southern and Eastern Hemispheres of the globe—it carries the bittersweet taste of hope from a flourishing and vital Christian faith with the sorrowful history of colonialism and cultural genocide: joy in the midst of tragedy. Mission carries the same uncertainty that the father of the possessed son experienced when he declared: "I believe; help my unbelief!" (Mark 9:24).

Because mission imports such conflicting meanings, it is crucial for us to gain some historical and theological perspectives that will provide us with a critical foundation for our conversations. Moreover, we need to explore the context from which many of these meanings emerged, and to suggest some theological connections that will speak to Christians in the United States.

As stated in the introduction, this chapter offers an important theological lesson from missiology. When reflecting on our missional task, Christians in North America need to be aware of the *contextualized* character of the gospel. This means that the church needs to take seriously how the cultural, economic, social, political, and religious situation of its context shapes its understanding of the gospel and its missional task.

Frequently, however, it is difficult for Christians in North America (and in any other context) to discern and discover the contextualized character of the gospel. Many Christians assume that their Christianity is normative and pure; they are blind to the interplay between the gospel and their culture(s), the ways in which their faith shapes and is shaped by the context where they live. There is no "pure" faith, and mission is always shaped by the context. Hence, the Christian faith is always a contextualized faith, and this contextualized faith is also what Christians share in their missional endeavors. The contextualized nature of the gospel is based on God's incarnation in Christ. Contextualization, as we will see in other chapters, is a natural process in both the transmission and the reception of the gospel.

An important question, nevertheless, is: How can Christians in a particular context become aware of their contextualized gospel, and therefore, also become aware of the methods used to share the gospel? An important resource for such an exploration comes from cross-cultural mission encounters. The critical assessment of the cultural other—those to whom our mission work is frequently directed—significantly contributes to identify cultural factors that shape our understanding and practice of the gospel and our mission work. Their assessment often serves as a "mirror" in mission. They help us see who we are as Christians in mission.

But why do we need a "mirror" for our mission work? We need the assessment of the cultural other because it helps us look critically at the ways in which our contexualized gospel—the gospel we also communicate—is either open and congruent with God's missional work or under cultural captivity, bound to human values and interests distant from the values of the Reign of God. Regrettably, many times our contextualization of the gospel is not as healthy as we might think and it needs the renewal of the Spirit of Christ, renewal that usually begins with a critical evaluation of our mission work from those who have been missionized. As a result, contextualization is not discerned in isolation from the people who live in the context where mission is being done. On the contrary, contextualization requires an intentional conversation—a conversation between the missionaries and the context, between the missionaries and the people in the context, between these people and their own context, and between the three parties and God. It is a multidimensional conversation in which missionaries become partners and facilitators, and provide cross-cultural insights in the process of contextualization.

What follows is an essential step toward an evaluation of the contextualization of the gospel and of mission in North America. This step focuses on the mission practice of congregations. It also helps us see how missiology and cross-cultural mission, as theological disciplines, can contribute to the liberation of the mission of the North American church from the captivity that restrains it.

The Captivity of Mission:
Five Mission Models and a Mission Framework
That Restrain Mission

The five mission models and the mission framework that follow are a description of the practice and theology of mission in many congregations. They are an appraisal of the understanding of mission from a church-based perspective. They serve as a map by helping us see and evaluate the situation of mission in local congregations, denominations, and parachurch organizations. As models and a framework, they are not fixed, nor do they exhaust reality. Despite their limitations, they may help us understand the obstacles and tensions regarding mission in congregations and organizations.

During my teaching and pastoral experience in North America, I have witnessed the struggle of Christians, especially mainline Protestants, in coming to terms with "mission." To talk about "ministry" is fine, but once we begin conversations about mission everything becomes blurred. To some extent, theological categories such as "evangelical," "ecumenical," and others have created barriers that impede dialogue regarding mission at local and grassroots levels. There seems, however, to be a *syndrome of ambiguity* when speaking about mission. Everybody seems to know what "missions" is about without trying to understand the essence of "mission." This *syndrome of ambiguity* restrains congregations from engaging in mission, thus making them captive to their own ambiguity.

1. The first and most common model of mission is *mission as an overseas task*. On the one hand, mission is done for those unsaved and unchurched in the distant lands of Africa, Asia, Latin America, or the Pacific. It is the task for the salvation of the "heathen," and the civilizing of the "savage." Mission is to be done "out there," not "in here." It keeps a very clear boundary between those who do mission—the subjects of mission—and those who receive mission—the objects of mission.

On the other hand, the model of *mission as an overseas task* takes another shape in Christian communities who claim a different relationship between those in the North Atlantic regions and those in the Southern continents. Framed under terms such as "partnership," "mutual dependency," and "learning from one another," *mission as an overseas task* usually continues to uphold a distance-learning attitude with very limited educational and missional structures to help the "learning of the other" and the "partnership" to become an integrated congregational experience. Regrettably, the dynamics of those relationships continue to be dependent on structures that polarize the missionaries and the missionized; the developed and the undeveloped; the faithful and the religious; the rich, the middle class, and the poor—thus sustaining, though in a more sophisticated way, the object/subject of mission dichotomy.

Some of the effects of the *mission as overseas task model* are: (1) the inability to see the interconnection between the two different contexts; (2) the lack of theological and ethical reflection regarding the economic and social disproportion found among the partners; (3) the lack of congregational or institutional structure to translate the missional experience into the worship life of the community; (4) the lack of congregational or institutional guidance to help the communities find spiritual connection between the missional experience and daily life in their respective contexts and in their mutual relationship; (5) the tendency of the stronger partner in moving on to another partnership without a suitable decision-making process with the weaker partner and a proper closure that benefits a more informal relationship and future partnerships. Unfortunately, we continue to preserve similar patterns of old mission theologies and practices that are unacceptable for the twenty-first century.

2. The second description of mission in congregations, denominations, and parachurch organizations is "to identify and solve problems" for a community. This concept of mission reflects the North American cultural trait of seeking to provide an effective and practical response to the unexpected, the discomforting, and possibly the conflictual and/or the controversial situations in the life of the community. It becomes a maintenance and problem-solving activity. It is in reality little more than an administrative task with a theological nuance.

Christian communities that reflect this cultural trait assume that their programs contribute to the coming of the Reign of God. Mission becomes the communication of the gospel of Jesus Christ through the service of the Christian community. Hence, mission is a corollary of professional ministry within the rhetoric of the Reign of God and Christian service. Mission is searching for solutions to problems, allocating funds to keep programs running, creating a committee to discuss and propose avenues of engagement for a communal problem, and, for example, sponsoring a week of overseas ministries awareness to receive economic support from the congregation. It is going out and making things right! It is part of an insider/outsider frame of reference where the insider has solutions and the outsider has problems.

At a deeper level, this model of mission is the act of imposing, restoring, or establishing a notion of order perceived as vital by the missionary community or Christian experience. It is nurtured by a cultural characteristic of efficiency and productivity versus a context perceived as chaotic. I call this second description of mission the *efficiency model of mission.*

Let me give an example. In many places around the world, women come together to wash clothes at public faucets. These public faucets are a social and cultural location in a community where women come together to discuss issues. They are a place of gender support, mutual communication, communal planning, and in some cases, communal protection in times of war. To build a water system for such a community is definitely a contribution to the life of a community, and particularly to the lives of local women. However, the efficiency of bringing water to the home becomes a destructive factor in the social and cultural webs of women in that community. What is efficiency for one group of long- or short-term missionaries is disruptive to the social and cultural relations of a community. The *efficiency model of mission* assumes that the missionary culture comes to solve the perceived chaos of another community without considering the cultural configuration that is in place in that perceived chaotic culture. Efficiency and productivity replace careful study and engagement with the missionized cultures.

I have heard the argument that the urgency of material need should prevail over the time-consuming process of careful study and engagement with the missionized cultures. This has been a persuasive argument to promote projects that have been strongly supported by missionized groups in the context of developing countries. Nevertheless, it should not be a surprise for a group of missionized Christians not to be aware of the impact of such projects on their own people. It should not be a surprise either for this group of missionized Christians to suddenly discover that the projects have disturbed the cultural process and configuration of their people, creating other problems and giving the impression of lack of gratitude to their missionaries from overseas. Consequently, I want to suggest that the problems of the *efficiency model of mission* are not intrinsic to the projects themselves, but to the lack of awareness regarding the changes that technology and productivity—as simple as they may be—create in a particular context.

3. The third model for mission is associated with the nineteenth- and mid-twentieth-century formulas proposed by missiologists such as the German Gustav Warneck and the missionary statesman John R. Mott. This formula is a combination of global evangelism, Christian education, and Western civilization. This particular description of mission results in the indiscriminate use of the term "missions." As a result, when "missions" is mentioned, multiple meanings are evoked. For example, "missions" can refer to: (1) the sending of missionaries to a territory; (2) the activities that such missionaries undertake; (3) the agencies that sponsor the missionaries; (4) the non-Christian world or "mission field," or "mission stations." "Missions" also alludes to the propagation of the faith, the expansion of the Reign of God, the conversion of the heathen, and the establishment of new congregations.

It is common to find in these elements a driving motivation for church members to get involved in mission. Such a driving motivation comes, as Orlando Costas said, from "the interplay between the American missionary movement and American imperialism."[1] It nurtures a nostalgic vision of what American "misssions" was all about: the exportation of Euro-American Christianity and civilization as the good news of the gospel of Jesus Christ. This description of mission I call the *nostalgic model of mission*.

The passion found in the *nostalgic model of mission* is striking. First, the nostalgic model romanticizes past memories of a perceived time of glory and triumph. It is nurtured by the religious messianism that has so intensely shaped the identity of the United States—an elected country for the salvation of the world. It is linked to patriotism and cultural superiority, identity factors deeply ingrained in the North American psyche.

Any critical engagement with these formulas is considered to be a sign of disbelief and distrust of the "gospel of Jesus Christ." In many Christian congregations and organizations, to approve of these formulas is to be a legitimate Christian; to disapprove of them is to relinquish the faith. Furthermore, in many circles the *nostalgic model of mission* is a fundamental criterion for evaluating one's commitment to the Christian faith.

The *nostalgic model* experienced a crisis in the early 1970s. Churches in the Southern continents lifted their prophetic voices to denounce the imperialistic, paternalistic, and Westernizing character of some of the missionary activity. During this decade, a moratorium on mission and missionaries was declared in a significant number of Protestant churches, denominations, and missionary organizations, creating confusion and tensions between the "older" (missionary-sending, subjects of mission) and the "younger" (missionary-receiving, objects of mission) churches. For instance, it is not uncommon to see congregations that are captive to the *nostalgic model of mission* debating whether or not to send missionaries to countries where Christian churches have more vitality and missionary activity than congregations in North America. Moreover, the model continues to focus on activities and funding to help missionaries in the foreign field in a laissez-faire mode, which creates tensions among leaders of the "sending" institution. For sure, in the *nostalgic model of mission*, the congregation seldom participates in the missionary activity that it supports economically.

These tensions and dilemmas have pushed numerous churches and leaders to claim that mission cannot continue to be what it has been. Presently, though the *nostalgic mission* is strong in many Christian circles, the voice of change is increasingly making an impact on the lives of churches and communities, launching them to explore new avenues for mission theologies and practices.

4. The fourth model emerges out of the crisis of the *nostalgic model*. The consequences of the critical assessment of mission from the churches in the Southern continents generated confusion and uncertainty in some mainline Protestant churches in North America. As a consequence of the moratorium on foreign "missions," some churches and denominations decided to deny mission and be silent about it. Overwhelmed with guilt on the one hand, and witnessing drastic transformation in the ecclesiastical, economic, political, and religious world order on the other, the terms "mission," "missions," and "missionary," as Donald Messer states, "fell into disuse, disfavor, and derision."[2] Consequently, the fourth mission model arose: the *disappearing model of mission*.

The *disappearing model* silenced mission in many congregations. It simply did not exist in the theological and pastoral jargon of many Protestant communities of faith, and it had no meaning for their laity and leaders. The denial of the *nostalgic model* reached such intensity that mission seemed to disappear in many Protestant communities. Global mission committees became marginalized, "Global Missions Week" was erased from the regular programming of congregations, and terms such as "evangelism" and "mission" were exchanged for "outreach," "church growth," and "service."

5. The fifth model represents the opposite of the *disappearing model of mission*, for in this model, mission is everything and everywhere. Some who have kept the term "mission" in their church vocabulary have developed a view so comprehensive that everything becomes mission. As the late missiologist David Bosch wrote regarding this trend, mission is "everything God does as well as everything Christians believe they should be doing."[3] This fifth model is the *mission-is-everything model*.

The problem with the *mission-is-everything model*, according to Stephen Neill, is that when "mission is everything, mission is nothing." The naïveté of keeping such an understanding of mission in theological jargon results in diluting its critical, reflective, and practical dimensions. When mission is everything, rhetoric substitutes for action and commitment. Basketball in the church's gym is evangelism, and outreach becomes making people feel good about themselves. Theologically, planning replaces discernment, evil is an illusion, liberation is a utopia, and reconciliation becomes a program.

Mission in the West: A Missiological Framework for North American Congregations

During the last decade and a half, a new missiological framework has emerged among some North American missiologists and theologians. I want to briefly discuss this missiological framework because it (1) has taken the attention of significant church leaders, denominational executives, and theological faculties in the United States, Canada, and Western Europe, and (2) it has, in my opinion, provided a theological language with the potential of informing and shaping any mission model without making a significant change in the mission practices and theologies that emerge out of those models. I call this framework the *mission-in-the-West framework.*

The *mission-in-the-West framework* is informed, among other resources, by the missiology of the late Bishop Lesslie Newbigin, a distinguished leader in the missionary and ecumenical movements during the twentieth century, and continued by the Gospel and Culture Networks in the United States and Europe. The contribution of other North American theologians and biblical scholars has also shaped the missional framework. Both the Gospel and Culture Networks and these scholars have developed theological and missiological proposals addressing the needs of North American mainline churches as they face displacement and confusion in what they describe as a hostile, postmodern environment.

These missiologists and theologians have made an important contribution to the Christian mainline communities. First, they have rightly recognized and critically described the damaging legacy of Christendom in congregational and denominational life. Second, they have rightly proposed the end of Christendom in this century and the need to reinvent congregational life in the light of a post-Christendom era. Third, they have given biblical and theological language and perspectives guiding the churches in this

25

reinvention of the church, this "undiscovered country." Fourth, some have raised a prophetic voice naming the idolatry of the North American mainline churches with capitalism, wealth, and consumption. Moreover, a few have also called the churches to accountability regarding the poor and the disenfranchised in the North American context and the world. It is evident that these missiologists and scholars are seriously struggling to discern and guide the calling and sending of North American mainline congregations in a confusing environment.

I believe, however, that these missiologists and scholars fall short of including other critical issues in their analysis of the postmodern and post-Christendom era. For instance, in their literature, their conversation is focused on the "broader culture"; the culture developed and sustained by media, capitalism, consumerism, individualism, and the market economy, with almost no reference to the presence and interaction of other cultures with the "broader culture." Second, the main missiological issues are focused on the contemporary situation: the crisis of mainline congregations as they experience the loss of power and influence in North American culture. There is no analysis of the historical forces that, though at times assumed to have disappeared with Christendom, continue to give mainline congregations a certain level of power and influence in the North American context. Furthermore, some of these missiologists and theologians have replaced critical socioeconomic analysis with broad and general cultural reflections in a period when the gap between rich and poor has increased dramatically. In general, (1) their cultural analysis does not address the critical problems found in a society with a history and structures that help perpetuate injustice and repression; (2) their missiological proposals lack the awareness of a diverse Christian community and a pluralistic religious context; and (3) their missiological proposals lack differentiation from previous mission theologies and models that emerged within the influence of Christendom. From my perspective, as a missionized person, the proposals seem to keep Christian communities as the main protagonists of mission and to attempt to recover the religious and political influence lost in the postmodern era.

All of these mission models and the missional framework have common elements. Historically, they all emerged out of the spirit of the Protestant missionary movement of the nineteenth and twentieth centuries. They are either intrinsic to the movement or a result of further developments. As part of the movement, they agree on (1) the urgency of sharing the gospel with the world, and (2) the dream of a Christian and better world. As a development in the history of the modern missionary movement, they have in common an ambiguous response to the surprising consequences of (1) the spreading and appropriation of the gospel in the world, and (2) the surprising changes lasting into the twenty-first century.

The appropriation of the gospel by non-Westerners has created a *theological and missiological displacement* for Western theological and missiological thought and practice. Radical and unexpected appropriation of the gospel has gone beyond the "civilizing effect" expected by Euro-American missions. The maturity and Christian vitality of those for whom mission activity was done has been perceived in many mainline Protestant circles as both an achievement and a challenge to Western theological and missiological activity. Some of the challenges are either dismissed or put aside by North American congregations and missiologists. In a disturbing way, this dismissal can be interpreted as another way in which powerful "sending" congregations and institutions display superiority over those who they missionize. On the other hand, others, who frequently deal better with the *theological and missiological displacement*, appropriate and contextualize the missiological contribution from the non-Western world, making interesting connections and promoting intercultural relations.

Furthermore, the dream of a Christian and better world has collided with two world wars, Communist upheavals, the Cold War, Third World impoverishment and exploitation, revolutions, the birth of new nations, ethnic and religious movements, and increasing migration and urbanization. These and many other events and trends of the past century have created fear and uncertainty among many Christians, particularly Western Christians.

Regrettably, these mission models and this framework, shaped and developed within the missionary movement, restrain the church's capability to deal with the changes described above. Instead of engaging in critical and creative reflection regarding mission, many North American congregations are held captive by the ambiguities that have resulted, ironically, from their own missionary activity. Many congregations, for example, on the one

hand, feel that the best they can do is support and financially sponsor mission projects, while on the other, mission is just a black hole
at which they are hopelessly throwing money. Mission feels so distant, and yet it consumes some of the resources considered important for many congregations.

Second, these mission models and the *mission-in-the-West framework* share a tendency to overlook the increasing complexity and
challenges facing the church in mission settings today. As mentioned in the example under the *efficiency model of mission,* installing
faucets, schools, and churches is much more complicated than the
actual process of planning and building facilities. Global, regional,
and national conditions affect the lives of people more acutely
today than yesterday. Upward mobility, improvement in education, and the overcoming of poverty are not accomplished just by
doing projects. Reality is much more complicated than we may
wish to believe.

These mission models and framework overlook the cultural
complexities of cross-cultural and cross-class witnessing to the
gospel of Jesus Christ. These models are inclined to focus in
efficiency over transformation, membership and lifestyles over
conversion and discipleship, denial of accountability over facing
ambiguity and reconciliation, and triviality over responsibility.
Consequently, they have an inclination either to do mission within
a safe, comfortable, and protected setting, or to dilute mission
activity in such a way as to keep the stability and order of a community and/or church structure. The outcome is devastating: discernment and liberation are replaced by efficiency; newness of life
and faith are traded for a nostalgic past; repentance is substituted
by denial; dialogue, through fear, succumbs to isolationism, super-
ficiality becomes the way to exercise integrity; politeness works as
reconciliation. Such attitudes and approaches remove the church
from the life of the Spirit of Jesus Christ. Our communities and the
world have expanded in such a way that it is difficult yet urgent to
realize that the mission of God, *missio Dei,* goes beyond administrative efficiency, therapeutic nostalgia, guilt-driven denial, and
gullible openness.

Third, and particularly focusing on the mission models, they are
the result of the theological indifference of denominational and
theological institutions. There is limited opportunity to engage in
serious conversation regarding mission. As a result, congregations,

pastors, and lay leaders are captive either to the silence of theological circles or to nostalgic practices of mission.

At another level, these models separate mission from the life of the church. Mission becomes an appendix to the church's life in which only some members participate. Congregations are informed of their distant participation in "missions" only through an evening presentation of missionaries, or through a meal with some international person visiting the congregation. Fortunately, the *mission-in-the-West framework* is beginning to address the above issues by providing the missiological import in congregations, theological institutions, and denominational arenas.

If these models and framework depict to any extent the crisis in mission of many congregations, denominations, and parachurch organizations in North America, the questions are: (1) What can we do to change this mission practice? (2) Can we move beyond this captivity of mission? Missiology, as a theological practice, begins to provide insights and proposals by which local congregations can engage in mission. Missiology claims the missionary character of theology and the theological character of mission. It also claims that in order to be the church, the church needs to be in mission, because to be the church of Jesus Christ is to be in mission.

This generation of North American Christian leaders must face this challenge with integrity of faith and an openness of heart. Integrity of faith comes from a never-ending process of discernment of the presence of God's Spirit in the world. Openness of heart comes from God's exciting invitation to discover God's wonders in the world. With such a faith experience, our next step is to give witness to that which "we have seen and heard" (1 John 1:3). What follows are rich and diverse possibilities that will enable the Christian churches in North America to become missionary churches in many ways.

The next chapter explores different issues regarding Christian mission. I will explore Christendom's legacy on mission and provide a definition for mission that will help us discover a fresh understanding of mission for our context.

---

1. Orlando Costas, *Christ Outside the Gate* (Maryknoll, N.Y.: Orbis, 1982), 80-81.

2. Donald Messer, *A Conspiracy of Goodness* (Nashville: Abingdon Press, 1992), 21.

3. David Bosch, *Witness to the World: The Christian Mission in Theological Perspective* (Atlanta: John Knox Press, 1980), 15.

CHAPTER TWO

Mission Revisited

Christendom and *Missio Dei*

In this chapter I will discuss at length the significance of the term *mission*. As I indicated earlier, in the last few years theological reflection about the mission of the church has changed radically. Therefore, I propose that we begin by looking at the traditional understanding of Christian mission. After studying the traditional understanding, we will amplify the statements made in the introduction, marking the recent theological and missiological changes and their implications for the church.

Christian Mission and History

Christendom and Mission

Christendom is the fusion of a political structure with the Christian religion, beginning with the Roman Empire and continuing, though gradually diminishing, into the twenty-first century. The concept of Christendom has its origins in the decision of Emperor Constantine in the fourth century to support Christianity above all other religions of the Roman Empire. The Christian historian Eusebius of Caesarea, in his monumental work *Church History*, celebrates this integration of the political order of the Roman Empire with the Christian religion as *the* high point in the history of Christianity, the completion of the kingdom of God on earth.

One of the consequences of Christendom was to identify a particular geographic region—in the case of the fourth century, the Roman Empire—with a particular religion—Christianity. In time, most inhabitants of the Roman Empire understood themselves to be members of Christendom and therefore Christians—with the exception of the Jews, whose presence was intermittently tolerated. The geographic borders divided not only kingdoms but also religious loyalty and identity. Those groups, and later nations, outside the borders of the empire or of Christendom were not Christian and therefore were the objects of the mission work of the church. This geographical and religious configuration has shaped the understanding of mission significantly: mission is the evangelization of peoples who are not part of Christendom.

The religious-political construct of Christendom has formed and informed the missionary enterprise up until our day. Some of the theological and practical implications of the relationship between Christendom and mission are:

1. Mission is the activity of the church.
2. The mission of the church is an activity whose purpose is to expand the Christian faith outside the boundaries of Christendom.
3. Mission is a one-directional activity, from "Christendom" or "the center" to "outside of Christendom," or "non-Christian" territory.
4. Missionary activity consists in the proclamation of the gospel, the conversion of non-Christians, and the implementation of the political, cultural, and religious order of Christendom.
5. Non-Christian territory is the location of missionary action. "Ministries" exist within Christendom; "missions" exist outside of Christendom.

What are the consequences of these theological and practical implications for mission? First, *mission is the activity of the church.* The church, as part of Christendom, has received, is responsible for, and is the protector of the Christian faith and its political structures. The gospel has been granted and received, and now it is the church's responsibility to communicate it in order that it be known and accepted. God gave Christians the gospel; it is the church's responsibility to announce to non-Christians that which was given.

Second, *the mission of the church is an activity whose purpose is to expand the Christian faith outside of the borders of Christendom.* Mission is understood principally as an activity of the expansion of Christendom. Christian missionaries cross geographic and cultural borders in order that the Christian faith be expanded to groups of non-Christians, winning not only followers but also whole new geographic regions, as in the sixteenth century in the Americas. Even in the cases where Christendom had lost political power and its future was in danger, missionary work sought the expansion of the Christian faith and frequently had the intent of recovering lost land and political power, just as in the conquest of the Saxons by Charlemagne in the late–eighth and early ninth centuries or during the first crusade in the late–eleventh century.

Third, *mission is a one-directional activity, from "Christendom" or "the center" to "outside of Christendom" or "non-Christian territory."* The mission of the church, whose purpose is to expand the faith together with Christendom, is born, develops, and completes itself within Christendom. All the details pertaining to mission, the reasons for the expansion of the faith, the missionary strategies, the establishment of churches, the statutes that dictate the form in which converted peoples should conduct themselves, and the structures of church and political order *are already determined* by Christendom. Christendom is the promoter, executor, arbiter, and consummator of Christian mission.

Fourth, *missionary activity consists in the proclamation of the gospel, the conversion of non-Christians, and the implementation of the political, cultural, and religious order of Christendom.* The content of missionary activity has two dimensions, simply stated but difficult to achieve. First, the mission of Christendom is the proclamation and announcement of the gospel so that non-Christians may convert to Christianity. Although the methods to achieve the conversion of non-Christians have varied throughout the course of the history of "missions," the purpose has continued to be the same. Second, the conversion of non-Christians goes hand in hand with the implementation of the political, cultural, and religious order of Christendom. Therefore, mission is to establish Christendom in non-Christian territory!

Fifth, *non-Christian territory is the location of missionary action. "Ministries" exist within Christendom; "missions" exist outside of Christendom.* In the introduction, we referred to the word "missions" *as the activity that the church does to communicate the gospel to the unevangelized.* Therefore, "missions" is a word that evokes missionary activity, limited to non-Christian territories or within nominal Christendom (as we will see below). Faith activity, the life of the church, ordinances or sacraments, and congregational practices within Christendom or congregations are called "ministries." "Missions" is only for non-Christians in non-Christian lands. This implies that the church does not need mission: it is not the *object* of mission; rather, the church is always the protagonist, the *subject* in mission.

Protestant Christendom and the Crisis of Christendom

As I indicated above, Christendom has changed throughout history; it has had the capacity to adapt to the new contextual changes, without losing some of its core values. Interestingly, Protestantism threatened Christendom in a significant way during the sixteenth and seventeenth centuries. Ironically, Protestantism and Christendom also developed a mutual dependency sustaining each other as they faced the challenges of modernity. Thus, for a significant number of modern Christians, on the one hand, Christendom still exists despite its change, and on the other, they have an apprehension toward Christendom both in its Protestant and Roman Catholic versions.

The Protestant missionary movement of the nineteenth century had Protestant Christendom as its structure of support. Protestant Christendom, which some historians date to the seventeenth century, is the fusion between Christian faith in its Protestant version and the values of the modern world. There is no doubt that distinct Protestant groups have different levels of fusion with and acceptance of the values of the modern world. However, the compatibility between the different branches of Protestantism and the modern world is real. Protestant Christendom has understood mission as evangelization—conversion of pagans to Protestant Christianity—and civilization—the establishment of the values and lifestyles of the Western, Protestant, and Christian world in non-Christian lands. Some have strongly argued that Protestant Christianity also understood mission as the reformation of the Roman Catholic Church in Europe. The implications and consequences mentioned above, however, continue to be equally pertinent for Protestant Christendom and mission whether to non-Christian lands or to Europe.

In the United States and in Western Europe, Christendom—Catholic as well as Protestant—is in crisis. The church structures that guaranteed the stability and prestige of denominations have been disappearing. For instance, church official statements—encyclicals, pastoral letters, official documents—do not carry the same leverage that they once did. Congregants are more critical, at times more informed, and less inclined to accept the authority of these documents, even when they belong and participate in local church life. The churches already do not have the same appeal and the Christian population does not have the same loyalties that existed thirty years ago. New cultural propositions and a new concept of world order question the order of Western Christendom—even in its Protestant version, often considered the most compatible with the values of the modern world.

Other factors that have contributed to the crisis of Western Christendom are: religious pluralism, the erosion of traditional authority, the reduction of the power of the state, the missionary activity of other religions, cultural and ethnic diversity, and suspicion of traditional institutions such as the state, government, and church. For many people, these factors point to a crisis in the Christian faith, the structures of the church, and traditional values. This crisis means a loss of privilege for Christianity facing other religions. It means the loss of progress in the face of underdevelopment, the loss of the absolute in the face of relativity, and the loss of the hegemony of the rich in the face of the poor.

For Hispanic-Latino and Latin American people, Western Christendom is indeed in crisis. Roman Catholic Christendom is also in crisis as it tries to define and fight for legitimacy in the midst of the people. Hispanic-Latino Roman Catholic missiologists continue to assume certain values, structures, and characteristics of Roman Christendom, while at the same time proposing new avenues of mission work that are not totally compatible with Roman Christendom. In Latin America, the Latin American Episcopal Council (Roman Catholic) continues to discuss the significance of the "New Evangelization" as a strategy for preserving Christendom and the values of the Christian faith without losing momentum in the contemporary world.

Among Hispanic-Latino and Latin American Protestants,

evangelicals, and Pentecostals there is already a type of ambiguity, for on the one hand, we are descendants of Catholic Christendom, as a result of the predominant Spanish and Portuguese colonization, and on the other hand, we have appropriated many of the values of Protestant Christendom—progress, individualism, and so forth. Regardless of our level of acceptance or rejection of Protestant Christendom, non-Catholic Christians continue to practice mission within the framework of Western Christendom. We evangelize the nonevangelized, we evangelize the nominal Christians (Roman Catholics and evangelicals), and we evangelize Christians whose practices are identified as syncretistic with paganism. We then incorporate converts into a micro-Christendom—a type of communal civilization—in our congregational and denominational structures. Mission continues to be a one-way activity—people moving from the world to the church, from ignorance to civilization, from non-Christian to Christian identity and existence.

The Protestant and Evangelical Missionary Legacy

Mission and Salvation

Above I indicated that the implications and consequences of Western Christendom for mission are compatible with those of Protestant Christendom. However, the practice of mission in Protestant circles is distinct from that of the Roman Catholic and Orthodox traditions. For the purpose of this section, we will present two theological themes of the Protestant missionary legacy that clearly continue to influence the role of congregations in "missions" today.

The first theme is *mission and salvation*. One legacy of Protestantism interprets salvation as *a* gift of God that is granted in a moment in life, that is to say, conversion. This legacy, a development in the amalgamation of different theological resources, such as scholastic Calvinism, fundamentalism, evangelicalism, and neo-orthodoxy, often reduce salvation to two points in time. The first is the death and resurrection of Jesus Christ, the unique event of salvation and universal revelation. The second is the experience of conversion, the particular moment in which the revelation of God in Jesus Christ is given to a particular human being.

36

The theological principles that inform this theology of salvation and thus greatly influence the practice of "missions" are:

1. *Salvation is a gift of God.* Salvation, the human benefit of the death and resurrection of Jesus, comes only from God. No human action can obtain it. To suppose that salvation can be obtained through human activity signals the sinful character of such activity. Salvation is the revelation of God in Jesus Christ and therefore is given only by God.

2. *Salvation is tangential to the history of humanity.* The salvation or revelation of God in Jesus Christ happens in history but lies outside history. M. M. Thomas, in his book *Risking Christ for Christ's Sake,* characterizes Karl Barth's understanding of salvation and history with the following metaphor: "As a tangent touches a circle, without touching it, so does the revelation of God in Jesus Christ touch history, without touching it."[1] Salvation happens in history, in the event of the crucifixion and resurrection of Jesus, but its effects transcend history, leading to a transcendental understanding of God and to eternal life.

3. *Salvation in Jesus Christ marks a discontinuity with the world.* The beginning and ending point of the Christian faith is the revelation of God in Jesus Christ on the cross at Calvary. Once the human being receives this revelation and accepts salvation in Jesus Christ, there is a rupture between the world and sin. This revelation is in absolute discontinuity with the world, other religions, and all human activity that pretends to search for salvation or truth.

4. *The church is the community of "redeemed sinners" that are in, but not of, the world.* The church of Jesus Christ has the revelation and knows the truth. It is in the world and therefore subjected to temptation and sin, but because it has the revelation of God, the church has the opportunity to repent, convert itself into a community of "redeemed sinners," and continue to proclaim the gospel.

5. *The church is responsible for proclaiming the truth of the revelation of God in Jesus Christ, for proclaiming the gospel for the conversion of all human beings.* Given that the church has the knowledge of "the mystery of salvation," the church is the protagonist in missionary activity. This missionary activity has two themes. First, it is intertwined with the Second Coming of Christ, the *parousia.* When the gospel is preached to all the corners of the earth, the church will fulfill the requirement for the Second Coming of Christ. The urgency of preaching the gospel flows from the conviction that

Christ will come again soon, when the task of evangelization is complete.

Mission as Civilization

The second theme is *mission and civilization*. The Protestant missionary legacy assumes the responsibility of "giving a new cultural programming" to the evangelized. The relationship between "missions" and "civilization" is evident when we observe that missionary work is often accompanied by educational work, whose purpose it is to create a Protestant or Christian ethic, such as the work ethic, within the new context. This has been true, for example, in the case of Protestant missionary work in Latin America and the Caribbean. Missionary agencies and boards have invested grand efforts in evangelistic and educational work with the purpose of changing and improving the lifestyles of the evangelized.

This second theme, as I will discuss below, nuanced the theology of salvation described above. The church's mediation of salvation seemed broader and comprehensive given the civilizing missionary responsibility. The integration of mission into both salvation and civilization began to diversify mission practices and theologies in the nineteenth and early twentieth centuries. However, both continue to be legacies that inform our mission practice and theology today.

Some of the implications of the relationship between mission and civilization in missionary territory are:

1. *The perception is that the culture or context where "missions" occur is backward or lacking, in the best cases, and "pagan" or "demonic" in the worst cases.* When the culture of the missionary territory is perceived to be backward, this establishes an inequality between the mission agents and the people in the territory. The missionary agents exhibit a tendency toward cultural superiority. In cases in which the culture is perceived to be "pagan" or "demonic," the missionary work tries to extract the nonevangelized from this culture. In both cases, it is very common to assume that the cultures of the nonevangelized are the cause for their backwardness and the stagnation of progress in their culture.

Even the few missionaries with exceptional understanding of other faiths and cultures, such as the Scottish missionary John Nicol Farquhar (who engaged in interfaith dialogue with Hindus and wrote *The Crown of Hinduism,* one of the most important books on Christian-Hindu encounter early in the 1900s, and still used today), argued that non-Christian faiths, though rich and God-given for a particular culture in history, lacked the necessary structure for engaging in the modernizing endeavors of a world in progress. Other faiths, such as Hinduism and Buddhism, did not have the resources to help a people develop the needed human understanding and vision to move into the progress of a new world order.

2. *The demand upon the new convert is that she or he will exhibit discontinuity with her or his culture.* It is expected that the new convert, upon accepting the Christian faith, will break with the lifestyles, the cultural and religious practices, and the standards of conduct of the society in which he or she lives. The best testimony of salvation is radical discontinuity with his or her culture.

3. *The new "Protestant" culture replaces the culture of the new convert.* The educational projects that accompanied the evangelism and mission programs have the purpose of filling the cultural vacuum resulting from the new convert's separation from her or his "pagan" or "sinful" culture. Through a process of "civilization," the missionaries teach each new convert the standards of conduct of the new Christian faith. Normally these new standards are antagonistic to the normative standards of the culture. This places the "Protestant" culture in confrontation with the "pagan" or non-Christian culture.

4. *The new "Protestant" culture is the culture of Western Christendom.* It is very common for the missionaries who train the new converts to assume that "Protestant" culture is that which emerges from the Bible. However, today we know that the "Protestant" culture we have learned corresponds with the values of Western Christendom. In many cases, education tries to create "photocopies" of the cultural standards that characterize Protestant and Western Christendom.

5. *With the erosion of Western Christendom, the "Protestant" culture that is transmitted is normally the culture of the missionaries, the denominational culture and/or the culture of the missionary agency or board.* New groups involved in "missions" do not come from the "Christian nations" of the United States, England, Germany, Holland, and so forth, but rather come from Third World countries such as Brazil, Korea, and India. Therefore, despite its large Western influence, the culture transmitted as "Protestant" civilization by these agents of "missions" is filtered through the cultures to

which they belong, or through the cultures of the denominations to which they pertain.

Moreover, though the largest numbers of missionaries continue to come from what was called "Christian lands," many of these missionaries have a different outlook, a different vision of mission work that is more grounded on cultural relativism, historical awareness, knowledge of other religions, and cross-cultural dynamics, which render a different transmission of the gospel in their mission work.

Keep in mind, however, that many of these theological principles and implications are indeed important missiological principles that should be maintained, as we will see in other chapters, but contextualized for this century. For instance, *salvation is a gift of God* for all creation. This is a unique and foundational Christian statement. However, as it will be discussed in chapters 4 and 5, salvation today is understood in broader and communal ways—different from the understanding proposed by Christianity in the Middle Ages, and from how it was understood until very recently. Consequently, it is crucial to keep in mind that some of the principles have relevancy today, but need to be differentiated and nuanced for the new contexts where the gospel of Jesus Christ is taking root.

Summary

We can observe that the consequences described above in relation to Christendom and mission are compatible with the Protestant and evangelical missionary legacy. For example, (1) *mission is the activity of the church;* (2) *the mission of the church is an activity whose purpose is to expand the Christian faith outside the borders of Christendom;* (3) *this mission is one-directional, from "Christendom or "the center" to "non-Christendom" or "non-Christian" territory;* (4) *this missionary activity consists of the proclamation of the gospel, the conversion of non-Christians, and the implementation of the political, cultural, and religious order of Christendom;* (5) *this non-Christian territory is the location of missionary activity.*

Although it may appear that this Protestant missionary legacy is most preoccupied with the salvation of souls, given its particular focus on the theology of salvation, in practice, both Catholic and Protestant missionary activity assume certain common principles with all types of Christian "missions." These principles are:

40

1. *The church is the beneficiary of the grace granted in the death and resurrection of Jesus Christ.* The church claims "to know" salvation through its knowledge of the salvific action of God in Jesus Christ.

2. *The church understands itself as the initiator and sustainer of missionary activity.* God has done God's part; now it is the church's responsibility to complete the "Great Commission" (Matthew 28), baptizing and making disciples of all nations.

3. *The church understands itself as an "institution of salvation."* Cyprian's phrase, "salvation outside the church does not exist," indicates this missional and ecclesial understanding. To accept that the church is the institution of salvation is to develop a mission theology and practice in which the protagonist of all missionary activity is the institution. Although one can make theoretical distinctions between the church as God's institution of salvation and the church as the institution of salvation, the history of missions signals that there is a strong tendency to play the role of God in missionary efforts. In this ecclesiastical protagonism, the activity of God becomes secondary. God has given salvation in Jesus Christ. As it is the church's responsibility to communicate and proclaim the gospel, traditionally the church has "made the decisions" about how to administer the economy of salvation.

4. *All missionary activity is one-directional, toward "the pagans, nonevangelized groups or Christian groups in need of renewal."* Mission is the expansion of Christianity and its structures to non-Christian places. When mission is instead done in Christian places, it seeks the renewal of the church or the correction of a corrupt Christianity in that territory. Mission only goes in one direction!

5. *Mission also consists in the transmission of "Christian" cultural values, which are normally opposed to the cultural values of the missionary territory.* In the history of missions, this transmission of "Christian" values has included the values, structures, and standards of Christendom, whether Catholic or Protestant. Today, in the face of the erosion of Western Christendom, many of the values that are transmitted are the legacy of Christendom incarnated in the cultural values that pertain to the mission agents, the denominations of the mission agents, or whatever the mission agencies and boards understand Christian values to be.

As I indicated above, Christendom is in crisis. Given the relationship between Christendom and mission, there is also a crisis in the theology of Christian mission. Mission cannot continue to be guided by some of the theological and missional principles discussed above. The voices of Christian people in "mission territories" have contributed new perspectives to the theology of Christian mission. As we continue, we will present some of these perspectives, some new foci, to help us create a missionary activity centered on God, the agent of mission *par excellence*.

Christian Mission for the Twenty-first Century

"Mission Is to the Church What Combustion Is to Fire"

The words of theologian Emil Brunner, "Mission is to the church what combustion is to fire," communicate that there is no church without mission.

Diagram #1

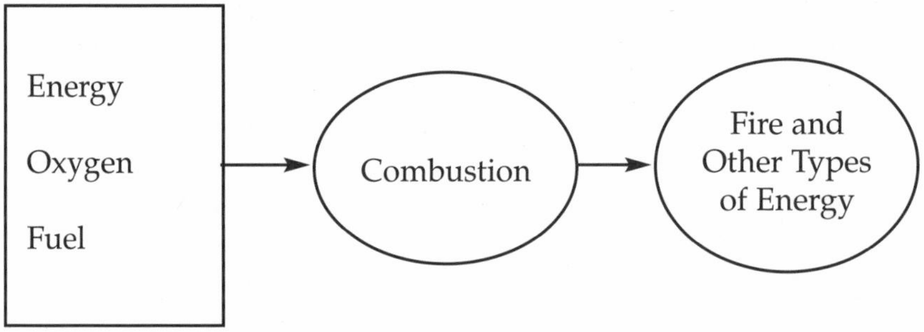

```
┌──────────────┐
│  Energy      │          ╭─────────────╮          ╭─────────────╮
│              │          │             │          │  Fire and   │
│  Oxygen      │ ───────▶ │ Combustion  │ ───────▶ │ Other Types │
│              │          │             │          │  of Energy  │
│  Fuel        │          ╰─────────────╯          ╰─────────────╯
└──────────────┘
```

Just as there is no fire without combustion and no combustion without the chemical reaction between the elements mentioned above, neither is there a church without mission nor mission without the activity of the Triune God. In other words, the Triune God initiates and participates in mission, and the Triune God creates the church and other expressions of God's mission. There is no mission without the activity of God. Mission and the church depend on God, just as combustion and fire depend on the chemical reaction between oxygen, fuel, and the "spark."

This metaphor uses the process of combustion to indicate the *continual* and *transformational* character of God's mission. There is combustion as long as the reaction continues between the elements; there is fire as long as combustion continues. Therefore, there is mission as long as God is active in the world, and a church as long as there is mission. In this process of reaction, combustion, and fire, transformation of energy occurs, just as God's mission is one of continual transformation.

The metaphor suggests, among other things, that the church is an object of God's mission. This implies that the church exists both because of and for God's mission. The church is not the protagonist of missionary activity. Rather, the church is as much an object of God's mission as is the world. The centrality of God in mission replaces the privileged character of the church in Christendom. Just as combustion produces and sustains fire, God's mission produces and sustains the church.

Fire is *one* of the products of combustion. Fire serves as a "constant spark" that maintains the chemical reaction between the fuel and the oxygen, creating combustion. But combustion simultaneously creates other types of energy such as light. The different types of energy produced by combustion are related, for the laws of physics indicate that energy is neither created nor destroyed, only transformed. Therefore, God's mission has distinct expressions that turn out to all relate to one another.

Diagram # 2

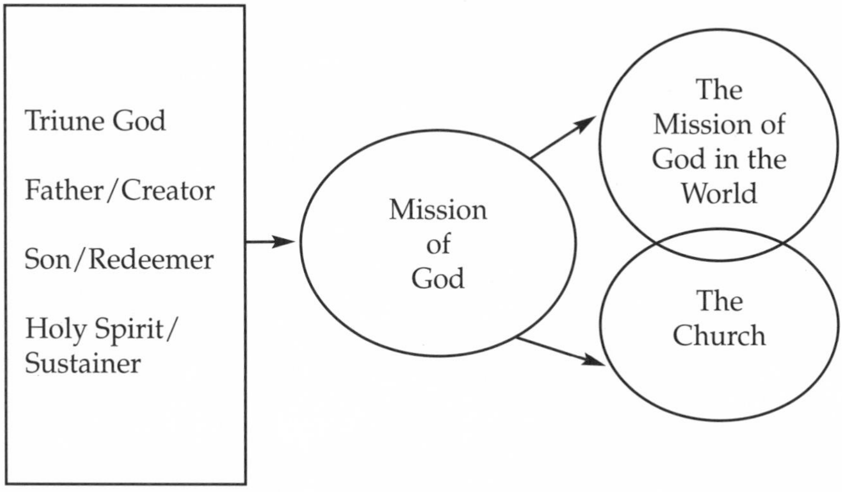

Just as fire is but one of the results of combustion, the church is only one of the results of God's mission. However, given that God's mission gives birth to the church, the church occupies a privileged place: that of coparticipation in God's mission. Just as combustion produces fire, contributing to sustaining combustion and creating other types of energy, the church participates in God's mission by being created by God's mission and coparticipating in God's mission. This means that the church is a *subject* as well as an *object* of God's mission.

Moreover, the world is also *subject* and *object* of the mission of God. God's missionary activity is manifested in the world, even if the church is either blind to such activity or, because of its own self-interests, disregards God's grace in creation. Just as many run away from fire and the by-products of combustion, at times many Christians have also run away from their religious responsibility of witnessing and celebrating God's doings in the world. The world never experiences the absence of God's activity and solidarity. Even in times of deep suffering, Christians should learn to trust that God is not silent, but rather present in solidarity and resistant to the ways of evil and destruction.

Mission, like combustion, is a process. The church, as an object and subject of mission, is immersed in an experience that requires a process of discerning and participating in God's missional activity. This discernment and participation is not a given, static imperative or reality. God's mission activity unfolds in history and finds its way in the midst of the turmoil and the ambiguity of the world. As it unfolds, God faces the fragility of creation and the reality of evil, the strength of hope and resistance of good. Because mission is a process, the church needs to develop a spirituality of mission, learning to discern, discover, participate, be patient, and be dependent on God's grace. A process requires time, and in Christian terms, time has an eschatological dimension. We Christians always live in the end times, in the coming of the Reign of God.

As God gives birth to the church as the Christian faith community, the church is the object of God's mission. As the church grows in and through God's mission, it is also the subject of God's mission. As God continues to act in the world, the world is also the object and subject of God's mission. How is the church different from the world? This important question will be discussed in the following chapter. Meanwhile, let's look carefully at the simple definition of mission provided in the introduction and discover some important theological nuances for our discussion.

What Is Christian Mission?

In the introduction, we looked at this definition: *Mission is the participation of the people of God in God's action in the world.* Now we shall delve into it further.

Mission is the participation . . . This phrase indicates that mission is not a mental state, or a desire or aspiration, or an activity of reflection or planning. Mission is "to participate," that is, to take an active part in the job another is doing. It implies uniting oneself with another or others to complete a task or determined action; it is to share in completing a job.

In the introduction, we talked about the relationship between the Father and the Son sent into the world. It is evident that the mission of God the Father is tied to the sending of the Son. The redemptive mission of God is carried out through the participation of the Father and the Son in the history of salvation. The Gospel of John most clearly captures this "mutual participation":

> Then Jesus cried aloud: "Whoever believes in me believes not in me but in him who sent me . . . for I have not spoken on my own, but the Father who sent me has himself given me a commandment about what to say and what to speak. And I know that his commandment is eternal life. What I speak, therefore, I speak just as the Father has told me." (John 12:44, 49-50)

The missional relationship is not limited only to the Father and the Son, for there is also a "mutual participation" in mission with the Holy Spirit. John 14:15-26 gives evidence of this relationship. Moreover, John 14:26 binds the three persons of the Trinity with the church in "mutual participation" in the search for truth: "But the Advocate, the Holy Spirit, whom the Father will send in my name, will teach you everything, and remind you of all that I have said to you."

It is evident that the New Testament gives testimony of the "participation" of the community of the Triune God—God the Creator, God the Redeemer, and God the Sustainer—in mission. Since God is the primordial agent of mission, mission is thus *an event in and of community*. God's mission is a participatory and communal activity among Godself.

Of the people of God . . . This phrase answers the question, *Who participates?* Mission gestates within the community of the Triune God, whose mission creates the church and gives it a privileged place in God's mission. The church is not the protagonist of mission, and therefore does not establish the objectives or the fundamentals of mission, but rather the church is a *subject* of God's mission. Therefore, the church lives in two realities: it is born out of God's mission and it participates in God's mission.

The church is the people of God, that community of children, adolescents, women, and men who worship God in gratitude for God's gifts. The church is also the community that proclaims, in multiple forms and symbolic ways, the myriad meanings of the gospel of the Kingdom. The church is renewed in this missional participation. Just as combustion is a continual process of transformation, the participation of the people in God's mission transforms the church.

In 1 Peter we can observe this double identity of being a people formed by God's mission and chosen to participate in God's mission:

> But you are a chosen race, a royal priesthood, a holy nation, God's own people, in order that you may proclaim the mighty acts of him who called you out of darkness into his marvelous light. Once you were not a people, but now you are God's people; once you had not received mercy, but now you have received mercy. (1 Peter 2:9-10)

Only as much as we discern, understand, and proclaim the virtues of the One who called us, can we call ourselves the people of God.

God's action in the world includes much more than what happens in the church. God is involved in all human history. The Reverend Mortimer Arias, a Latin American missiologist, expresses God's action in the world in this beautiful stanza of his hymn "In the Midst of Life":

> *You (God) are in the joy and you are in the pain,*
> *You share with your people in the struggle for the good.*
> *In Christ you have come, life to redeem,*
> *And as a pledge of your kingdom, the world to convert.*[2]

We should note that the missionary activity of conversion is of God and not of a human institution. The church proclaims and incarnates this action of God in the world in its preaching, in its worship, and in its missionary participation with God.

God's action in the world establishes another important theological theme of mission: eschatology. Eschatology is the theology "of the final things" or "of the last days." Another way of understanding eschatology is to think of *God's insertion into human history.* God's missionary activity in the world is eschatological, it proclaims that we live in the "last days," that we live in a time radically different from chronological time.

To take *God's action in the world* seriously, we have to live conscious of and advised that God, through the Holy Spirit, works in the midst of the life of peoples. Therefore, the church is called *to discern God's action in the world and to participate in God's mission.* Redemption, liberation, and God's reconciliation with creation in Jesus Christ are not suspended in the past in order to have an effect in the present. These actions of God are not just tangential to human history. They are incarnated—in the church and outside of the church—transforming the present and fertilizing the future with hope. God in Jesus Christ and through the Holy Spirit *acts in the world and accompanies God's people in God's mission.*

From this dynamic of people's participation with the missionary God, the *relational* character of mission is born. The relationship among those who send (the Father and the Son), those who are sent (the Son and the disciples), and the world (the space of God's missionary activity) is a net, a lobster trap, where the events and happenings in the world are united with God's missionary action. Consequently, the church that rejects the world rejects the space in which God's missionary activity occurs. The church that participates in God's mission in the world incarnates itself in the world to be a sign of the gospel of the Kingdom (as an *object* of mission), to discern God's missionary activity outside its institutional reality, and to be transformed, together with the world, through participation in God's mission (as a *subject* of the mission of God).

Summary: Criteria for a Christian Theology of Mission

1. *God is the main and most important protagonist of all missionary activity.* Mission is initiated, developed, and completed by God.

2. *Mission is a communal activity*. Mission begins with the participation of the three persons of the Trinity. It is initiated, developed, and completed in community.

3. *The people of God are both subject and object of God's mission*. God's mission gives birth to the church, and the work of God in the church is never complete. Simultaneously, the church also participates in God's mission. Without mission there is no church. Therefore, through its missionary participation, the church lives in continual transformation.

4. *God's missionary activity is in the world*. God is in relationship with the world, God's creation. God acts within human history offering symbols of liberation and reconciliation. God's missionary activity and incarnation in the world proclaim a new era, a new time. This is eschatology. The church is called to participate in the missionary activity of God in this new era of God. As God's missionary activity in the world transcends the church's institutional limits, the church's participation in God's mission is vital. In so doing, the church and the world shall be transformed.

The Bible is a fundamental resource for mission. The Bible has served as an inspiration and motivation, as a prescription for establishing strategies and content, and most recently, as a resource for developing a Christian theology of mission. The Bible has also been used to the detriment of God's mission. It has served as a companion and an enemy of mission. The next chapter explores the use of the Bible in the history of Christian mission and the most recent proposals for developing a biblical theology of mission.

---

1. M. M. Thomas, *Risking Christ for Christ's Sake* (Geneva: WCC Publications, 1987), 51.

2. Mortimer Arias, "En Medio de la Vida" ("In the Midst of Life") in *Cáliz de Bendiciones: Himnario Discípulos de Cristo* (St. Louis: Christian Board of Publication, 1996), p. 375. The translation is my own. Used by permission.

CHAPTER THREE

The Bible and Mission

Mission and the Interpretation of the Bible

The Bible has been an indispensable resource in the mission of the church throughout the ages. However, its use and interpretation has varied throughout history. In this chapter, I will first explore four models of biblical interpretation that have been used in missionary work. These models, as in chapter 1, will help us understand the development of the use and interpretation of the Bible in mission fields and in the discipline of missiology. Second, I will propose some themes or rubrics of interpretation emerging from the Hebrew Bible (Old Testament) and New Testament that have shaped and continue to shape the development of a biblical theology of mission. I will conclude the chapter with my contribution to the *biblical missional hermeneutic or interpretation* by considering the challenge of religious pluralism for today's mission. These themes testify to the vitality of the relationship that exists among the mission of God, the people of God, the Scriptures, and the context—the economic, cultural, political, religious, and social conditions of a region—where the mission of God manifests itself.

The Model *from the Center*

The first model is biblical interpretation *from the center*. This model is connected to the term "missions" discussed in the introduction and in the first chapter. The *center* is the church, or Christendom, the location from which missionary activity

49

emerges. This model of biblical interpretation limits the biblical witness to three dimensions: (1) the Bible is the book that justifies missionary work; (2) it is a type of recipe book with prescriptions to follow for accomplishing mission; and (3) it does not acknowledge the context of the interpreter, whether she or he may be a missionary or a missionized person. The biblical interpretation *from the center* assumes that the Bible pertains uniquely and exclusively to the church or missionary institution, and particularly to the agents of mission (missionaries). The purpose of this model is *to find in the Bible motivations, justifications, and strategies for doing mission.*

An example of the use of the model *from the center* is the way in which Matthew 28:16-20, the Great Commission, is interpreted and used as an anchor for establishing a missionary method. The commands to "make disciples," "baptize," and "teach" are frequently stressed without any other theological or contextual consideration.

This biblical interpretation *from the center* places certain limits on the missional task of the people of God. First, it tends to limit the use and interpretation of the Bible to the missionaries. One knows beforehand what mission is, and then searches for references in the Bible. Second, the biblical interpretation can be transformed into a model of mission. As a consequence, one confuses the biblical witness with dogma; confuses the vitality of the Scriptures in the Spirit of Christ with human and institutional prescriptions and directions. This restricts biblical interpretation to the search for jobs, justifications, strategies, and solutions to problems in the missionary field. Third, biblical interpretation *from the center* does not consider the context of mission. An interchange between the biblical text and the culture, politics, economics, and social issues of the mission context does not exist. Consequently, the world is ignored as the place of the missionary activity of God. Finally, biblical interpretation *from the center* does not give voice to the people who are the object of the mission of God. This biblical interpretation is one-way: from the agents of mission to those who are the objects of mission.

The Model *from the Margin*

The second model is biblical interpretation *from the margin*. Whereas in biblical interpretation *from the center* the context is "unimportant," biblical interpretation *from the margin* grants context a prominent place. The missionary personnel describe and analyze the cultural, economic, political, religious, and social conditions of a place, giving priority, in the majority of the cases, to conditions of oppression, poverty, and marginalization. Then they look in the Scriptures for examples that (1) are analogous to the situations previously described and analyzed, and (2) justify actions and projects that alleviate the conditions. The purpose of this model of biblical interpretation is to permit *the conditions of the context to select the biblical texts that justify missionary activity.*

The use of this model is common in the writings of official documents of denominational, interdenominational, and ecumenical mission bodies and of some other mission agencies. Normally, these official documents begin by describing the context where mission occurs. Then, through the use of biblical texts, a theological relationship is established between the context and mission, and the missionary practice is justified in that particular context.

The model of biblical interpretation *from the margin* focuses its efforts on the analysis of the context and its relationship with the biblical text. Although it avoids this limitation of the model *from the center*, it has serious limitations of its own. For example, frequently the incorporation of the context in biblical interpretation is superficial because it lacks the use of the social sciences to propose a detailed analysis. Consequently, there is no *dialogue* between the biblical text and the context, but rather mere correlation. Second, the analysis of the context is used as an absolute criterion to investigate and select biblical texts for mission. This criterion of interpretation leaves the biblical text silent because it does not permit any other interpretation of the text or the context. It is a one-way street: from the analysis of the context to the mission work. The biblical text only illuminates the context and justifies an action, a mission effort. Finally, normally the analysis of the context is done by people that (1) are not part of the context, or, in the majority of cases, (2) are agents of mission and in solidarity with marginalized people. The participation of the people who actually experience marginality in their daily lives is minimal. These people and their context are only used as an example to justify the use of the biblical text and the missionary practice. As the missionized people's participation in the act of biblical interpretation and missional reflection remains passive, they continue to be an object of mission defined by a participation alien to their own marginality.

The Model of the *Hermeneutical* or *Interpretive Circle*

The third model of biblical interpretation, the *hermeneutical or interpretive circle*, emerged from Latin American liberation theology. Proposed by theologian Juan Luis Segundo, the *hermeneutical or interpretive circle* avoids some of the limitations of the models already mentioned. For example, the *hermeneutical* or *interpretive circle* takes context very seriously, but also uses other criteria to interpret the biblical text. The study of the context and the interpretation of the text are done in dialogue and solidarity with the marginalized people, who thus become the principle protagonists in the interpretation of the text.

The *hermeneutical circle* has five stages: The first is the analysis of reality. Using the social sciences, one interprets and formulates causes to explain the situation of oppression under which people live. Part of this is an *ideological suspicion* indicating that the situation of poverty and oppression is not the will of God, but rather caused by human beings and political systems. In the second stage, the Bible is read in relation to this analysis of reality. A *political* reading of the biblical text is done. The biblical text and reality engage in mutual dialogue from which a liberating *praxis* emerges. This liberating *praxis* is an imperative, a liberating, transforming practice that makes up the third stage and is the missionary act that the community can enact, in faith that God accompanies the people. The fourth stage is the experience of transformation that is born and develops from the liberating *praxis*. This liberating missionary action leads to a new reality that is then evaluated and studied in the fifth stage. The *hermeneutical* or *interpretive circle* is complete in order to begin anew, and the Scriptures take their place in the continual conversation with the context and the liberating *praxis*.

Another way to understand the *hermeneutical or interpretive circle* is to think of the method of *seeing, judging, and acting*, which also comes from Latin American liberation theology. It begins with "seeing" or describing the reality of the community and the reality described in the biblical text. After "seeing," it moves to "judging." This involves identifying the situations of oppression and marginality in the community, and proposing strategies informed by the biblical text to overcome the oppressive conditions. When these strategies are enacted, mission is done in and through a liberating practice, creating a new reality. This new reality requires a new description to complete the circle and to begin to "see" the new reality.

One of the most important contributions of this model to the field of missiology is the awareness of the accompaniment of God. Through this awareness, mission and biblical reflection about mission recover a dynamic and fluid nature that requires discernment and growth in faith. The first two models limit God's activity to the past. The *hermeneutical* or *interpretive circle* breaks this static understanding of the grace of God and clearly places the continual and renewing presence of God in history and in creation. There is only one history, and this is the history in which God is the principle protagonist. The missionary God invites us to accompany God in mission by discerning God's salvific action in the world and giving of ourselves to participate with God in that action.

Another important contribution of the *hermeneutical* or *interpretive circle* is the richness of biblical interpretation joined to missionary activity—the *praxis* of the church. The interpretation of the text is enriched by the testimony of God in the life of the people and by the experience of the people in the midst of their struggles and achievements in their context. The *relational* character of mission is present in this biblical interpretation and missionary practice. The Bible stops being a book of prescriptions *(from the center)* or examples that apply to a situation *(from the margin)* in order to be a fundamental resource in the discernment of the will of God in the history of people. The Bible accompanies the people in their act of participating in God's mission to the world.

Finally, the *hermeneutical* or *interpretive circle* emphasizes the active participation in missionary reflection and action of people who experience oppression and marginalization. The people participate with God in liberating and reconciling action; the people are subjects, in reflection and action, in the work of God in the world, and particularly in their own context.

However, this model of biblical interpretation also has its limitations. Frequently, the *hermeneutical* or *interpretive circle* often reduces biblical interpretation in the context of mission to sociopolitical situations or class struggle. Feminist theologians have incorporated the *hermeneutical circle*, broadening the method to issues of gender and sex orientation. In spite of the broadening of the model, few have used the *hermeuntical circle* for themes and issues related to ethnicity, culture, and religion. Furthermore, the model assumes a Christian context characterized by conflict and the need for change. It does not have the theoretical dimensions to consider much more complex situations such as religious conflict, ethnic wars, and other violent encounters that illustrate, among the issues at stake, different religious authoritative sources—for instance, the Christian Bible, the Qur'an, and so forth. Though it may serve, for a Christian community, as a method to interpret Scriptures with these issues in mind, it does not provide a theological framework for interreligious and intercultural encounters. It continues to be a method primarily *for* the Christian community.

The Model of the *Missional Hermeneutic:* Initial Questions and the Missional Tapestry

A fourth model of biblical interpretation emerges from the theological and biblical dialogue between biblical scholars and missiologists. This model reflects a more mature stage because the biblical scholars take seriously the biblical witness in relation to mission, and the missiologists overcome the limitations of the previous models by discovering, with the aid of biblical scholars, a great missiological richness in the Scriptures. Both disciplines demonstrate interest in the biblical field by identifying criteria and questions that illumine and contribute perspectives to the development of a biblical theology of mission. I call this model the *missional hermeneutic*. Its purpose is *to discover in the biblical text the distinct perspectives of God's mission and God's peoples' participation (or lack thereof) in order to help us discern and continue to participate in the mission of God in our days.*

This model guides the reader to find central themes in relation to the mission of God and God's people in the whole of the biblical text. Therefore, it widens the selection of texts, attempts to overcome the exclusive and unbalanced dependence on context—whether the context where missionaries originate or the context where missionaries are working—and resists the reduction of missionary themes to sociological and conflict-oriented categories. Consequently, it allows the reader to discover the breadth and depth of the mission of God and God's people throughout the biblical witness.

Taking seriously the contribution of the social sciences to interpret and understand the biblical and missional contexts, the interpretation of the text begins with a conversation around the following questions: (1) Why mission? (2) How is mission done? (3) What is mission?

The first question explores the missionary character of God and the human/creation condition. On the one hand, *Why mission?* seeks to discover the character and nature of God in relation to creation's need, whether in need of liberation from oppression, of discipline to be restored, or of celebration for its liberation. The reference point is God's nature and character, God's relationship with God's creation. On the other hand, God's relationship with God's creation speaks of the condition of creation. If God is acting as a liberator, God's creation is in bondage (the Exodus story); if God's mission is reconciliation, then God's creation is isolated, marginalized, but restored (2 Corinthians 5:11-21); if God's action is unjust, then creation claims its own righteousness (Job); if God is confused and demanding obedience, then creation is not upholding the covenant. The nature and character of God's mission is a "mirror" for the human/creation condition.

Instead of using the question *Why mission?* the Catholic missiologist Robert Schreiter calls this missional question "the Bible for mission." Giving a different angle to my previous explanation, Schreiter proposes that the church search the biblical witness for the nature of the call to mission, the character of the divine command, and the origin of the relationship among the missionary God, God's missionary people, and the world.[1] For instance, in Jesus' words in John 20, the nature of the call for mission, the character of the divine command, and the relationship of the senders with the world are *relational*. As a result, the statement to the disciples, "As the Father has sent me, so I send you" (John 20:21), is more than just a command; it is a statement that carries the character of God's mission for the world, and the way in which God's people, as people sent, should relate to the world.

The second question explores the "how" of mission. Its attention still centered on the text, it serves as a bridge between the why of mission and the missionary act. The question brings to light the following: (1) the coherence or incoherence between the nature of God's mission and God's missionary act; (2) the coherence or incoherence between the missionary acts of the Christian community and God's missionary nature; and (3) who we are and what we do as missionaries. The question *How is mission done?* finds an important answer in Philippians 2:5-8:

Let the same mind be in you that was in Christ Jesus, who, though he was in the form of God, did not regard equality with God as something to be exploited, but emptied himself, taking the form of a slave, being born in human likeness. And being found in human form, he humbled himself and became obedient to the point of death—even death on a cross.

The "how" of the mission of the church ought therefore to reflect the nature and mission of the Triune God. The "emptying" of God in Jesus Christ becomes the bridge between the nature of God's mission and God's missionary act. The nature is consonant with the act. As the Christian community seeks to answer the question *How is mission done?* it needs to ask (1) Is God's mission consonant with God's missionary activity? (2) Is our mission, as coparticipants in God's mission, consonant with God's missionary activity? If it is not, how is it different? and (3) Who are we as God's missionary people? How does the way we do mission "read" who we are as God's missionary people?

The question *How is mission done?* also provides the church with an opportunity to explore conflicting themes about mission in the text. For example, the stories of Abraham, Sarah, Hagar, and Ishmael emphasize debate over human relationships, the distribution and responsibility of justice, and the biblical interpretation of God's covenants with, and promises to, Israel and other peoples—including the covenant with the Islamic people through Hagar and Ishmael (Genesis 16:11-16; 21:18-21). The examples of Jonah—where the expectations of the missionary are frustrated by a God of compassion who accepts the repentance of a pagan people and treats them as equal to Israel—and Ruth—a non-Jewish woman who enjoys the promises of the people of Israel to the point that she is included in the genealogy of Jesus—show how the plan and mission of God change and are enriched in history through the encounter between different groups of people. God appears as the protagonist of the events, interacting with biblical characters, and not as a facilitator or manipulator. Finally, Mark 9:38-41 and Luke 9:49-50 tell of the controversy that occurred among the disciples when they reported to Jesus that they had encountered a person casting out demons in Jesus' name, but "not following us." Jesus declares: "Whoever is not against us, is for us," indicating an openness to the missionary activity of God outside of Jesus' circle and his disciples.

Moreover, this question offers the opportunity to discover *what should not be considered mission.* For example, the story in Ezra 10 witnesses to the injustice that is done against foreign wives and the offspring of mixed ethnic marriages. Trying to preserve the ethnic and religious "purity" of Israel, foreign women and families are rejected, leaving them abandoned and without hope. The text establishes a serious conflict in the repercussions of the encounter between cultures and reflects an attitude of cultural superiority that affects the lives of the most vulnerable, the women and the children.

Unfortunately, many of these texts in Nehemiah and Ezra have been used to justify ethnic violence, cleansing, and even genocide. Other biblical texts also have been used to justify human and environmental atrocities. The bondage of literalism and the inability to self-criticize are critical factors for the many and damaging mistakes in our mission endeavors. Ironically, the Christian Scriptures are a rich testament of God's continuous call for God's people to be self-critical and to turn our ways to God's ways.

The New Testament is filled with examples in which traditional mission practices are questioned, abolished, and renewed by the Spirit of God. Some examples include the Sermon on the Mount, with its sayings framed by "you have heard it said … but I say to you…"; the stories in the book of Acts about the cultural requirements for accepting Gentiles into the Christian community (Acts 15); and the letters of Paul with their theological and missional struggles to discern the mission of God in new and challenging contexts (1 Corinthians 1:10-17). The question *How is mission done?* challenges the Christian community to read the Scriptures as a resource for discernment and analysis, more than as a recipe book or a book of instructions.

The third question, *What is mission?* begins with our missionary activity evaluating the content of our mission activity in light of Scriptures. Schreiter uses the phrase "the Bible in mission" to refer to this question. This question seeks to discover how the missionary activity of the Christian community witnesses to God's character and nature. As coparticipants in God's mission, does our mission give witness to the Triune God—as witnessed to in the Scriptures? Therefore, *What is mission?* can uncover our own interests and sinfulness *in our mission activity.*

Whereas the first question—*Why mission?*—explores the character, nature, and mission of God, and the second question—*How is mission done?*—looks for the consonance between God's missionary activity and the community's missionary activity, this third question goes deep into our mission activity, our *praxis*, as it helps us evaluate and change, in the light of Scriptures and with a fresh hermeneutic, our activity, so that it is closer to God's missional acts. Moreover, this question reminds the church of its continuous need for conversion and renewal, the character of being the object of God's mission.

This third question projects the historic character of the mission of God through God's people and the importance of the Holy Spirit in our need for repentance and new discernment of mission. In this sense, the "Bible in mission" is a partner in missionary activity, helping people discern and enact that which by the Spirit of Christ they discover to be the mission of God.

These three questions are not isolated from one another. We cannot answer one and then move on to another. Rather, the opposite is true. These three questions join in a biblical reflection that, without transferring biblical models to our day and conditions, allow creativity within the Christian tradition in light of the diverse circumstances and realities of each Christian community. This *missional hermeneutic* is a spiritual act of discovering God in mission—with the people of Israel and the church of the New Testament—and of discerning the church's action in the freedom of the Spirit to responsibly witness to the God of mission.

Some important resources that clearly show the use of the *missional hermeneutic* are Mortimer Arias's *Announcing the Reign of God* and *The Great Commission*, and John Driver's *Kingdom Citizens* and *Christian Mission and Social Justice*. Robert Schreiter's *Reconciliation* is a wonderful example of using the question of "the Bible for mission," of exploring the missionary activity of God's people vis-à-vis God's missionary nature. Lucien Legrand's work, *Unity and Plurality*, Donald Senior and Carroll Stuhlmueller's *Biblical Foundations for Mission*, and David Bosch's first section in *Transforming Mission* are titles that broadly use a *missional hermeneutic* to find the frequently lost relationship between Bible and mission in today's theological endeavor.

Elizabeth A. Johnson's work, *She Who Is*, tackles the nature, character, and mission of God from a feminist perspective. In answer to the question *Why mission?* Delores Williams, the distinguished African American womanist theologian, in her book *Sisters in the Wilderness*, offers a missional interpretation of liberation from the perspective of ethnic and gender oppression. Moreover, her engagement with the biblical text is a witness to sophisticated interpretation. Williams uses multiple resources, including non-Christian resources, and strongly denies certain texts that continue to serve as oppressive religious foundations.

In this same dimension, the reader can find in Justo González's work, *Santa Biblia* and *Out of Every Tribe and Nation*, and in Fernando Segovia's work on social location and biblical interpretation, rich and provocative insights and perspectives that keep the question of *How is mission done?* at the forefront of our missionary reflection and activity. Wesley Ariarajah's *The Bible and People of Other Faiths* is also an important text where *missional hermeneutics* are used with the challenge of witness to non-Christian people.

Most recently, however, the work of Walter Brueggemann, Stan Saunders, Charles Campbell, and others points to the challenge of mission in the Western context, focusing on the United States and affluent communities. Using the Scriptures and the ecclesial task of preaching, these colleagues struggle with a new reading of Scripture as it is juxtaposed with mainline congregation's practice and theology of mission.

Missiologist Charles Van Engen uses the image of a tapestry to integrate the *missional hermeneutic* with a biblical theology of mission. For Van Engen, the vertical threads of the tapestry represent the missionary activity of God, and the horizontal threads represent the response of the people of God to this activity. The biblical stories form a tapestry of the mission of God and of the life of the people. This *missional tapestry* is created when the vertical and horizontal threads unite, creating a fabric that encompasses God's activity and human response to that activity.

As we indicated above, the *missional hermeneutic* is a recent model. It was not until the first part of the twentieth century that missiology began as the systematic study of the relationship between the witness of the Bible and the mission of God. It was not until the first part of the twentieth century that the development of a biblical theology of mission began. We now turn to some important themes and approaches in the Hebrew Bible and New Testament that could enrich the way we try to answer the missional questions and, hence, contribute to the development of a biblical theology of mission.

The Hebrew Bible and Mission

The concept of mission in the Hebrew Bible differs from that of the New Testament. In fact, in the Hebrew Bible, mission is not specifically mentioned, but there is a concept of the universal rule of Yahweh and a sense of the mission of Israel. This concept shaped the understanding of the church's mission in the New Testament and in the biblical theology of mission that we see today.

1. *The universality in the Hebrew Bible.* Sometimes we commit the error of interpreting the Hebrew Bible in exclusive terms, only emphasizing God's preference for the Hebrew people. When the Hebrew Bible is interpreted in this way there is no place to see in it the point of departure for the missionary concept of the New Testament.

The Hebrew Bible is much more universal in its vision than is generally thought. For example, Genesis begins with a long prologue or introduction of eleven chapters in which the universal rule of the Creator over all of creation and all human beings is emphasized. The history of Israel that begins in chapter 12 of Genesis has to be understood within the general context of the history of humanity, and especially in light of God's purposes for humanity. Although the election of Abraham emphasizes the universal purpose of divine election, "In you all the families of the earth shall be blessed" (Genesis 12:3), this story is intertwined with other stories of God's missionary activity with people in conflict with, or excluded from, the tribe of Abraham and his descendants! All of this is to say that although Israelites are the chosen people of God, such an election is not a necessary mark of favoritism. Rather, it is better understood as a sign of obligation, the life required of a people living in covenant or alliance with God.

This responsibility for Israel, however, includes announcing its election in the midst of peoples that have other religions and, therefore, other salvation histories. The encounter of the faith and election of Israel with these peoples resulted in new understandings of how to live and express the election of God. At one extreme, there were strong confrontations such as that between Elijah and the prophets of Baal (1 Kings 18:20-40). On the other extreme, there were interesting interpretations of God's action, such as when Isaiah announced that the Persian king, Cyrus, would be a liberator of Israel (Isaiah 45).

In any case, Israel has a call from God to be a people of blessing for all the nations of the earth. There are multiple, enriching forms of expressing and enacting faith in Yahweh and his election. Without a doubt, through the diversity of the experience, on not a few occasions God intervenes to clarify for Israel their election. God uses the particular situations of the community to communicate God's will. At the same time, the people of Israel confront the challenge of discerning the will of God. It is in this continual dynamic that the people perceive the significance of their election and therefore their mission.

2. *The centripetal force of Israel's mission.* The Hebrew Bible depicts Israel's mission as more centripetal than centrifugal. It does not necessarily understand Israel as going to all the nations of the world to preach the message of salvation, but rather understands that all the nations of the world encounter their salvation in Israel. Therefore, Israel's mission is to witness to and announce God's salvation throughout all creation. Isaiah 53 and Psalm 2 confirm the centripetal character of Israel's mission:

> Now therefore, O kings, be wise; be warned, O rulers of the earth. Serve the LORD with fear, with trembling kiss his feet, or he will be angry, and you will perish in the way; for his wrath is quickly kindled. Happy are those who take refuge in him. (Psalm 2:10-12)

3. *From exclusivity to inclusivity: the stories of Jonah, Ruth, and Ezra.* The missionary character of the book of Jonah is well known, although we often miss the book's central message because we get so deeply involved in emphasizing that Jonah was swallowed by a big fish because Jonah did not want to go to Nineveh. The book of Jonah, however, is one of the most eloquent texts relating Israel's mission to the church's mission.

A careful reading will provide the core reflection about what was said earlier about God's purpose and Israel's universal mission. First, the purpose is not to call Israel to go into the world to preach the rule of Yahweh, but is rather a call to Israel itself to recognize that Yahweh's rule is universal. Therefore, the acknowledgment of

Yahweh's rule outside the geographic and ethnic limitations of Israel obligates the people of God to open their borders and recognize the grace of God in the life of peoples that accept the invitation to repent.

Second, this opening on Israel's part, personified in the person of Jonah, indicates how mission transforms faith and thought about the will of God. Jonah did not want to go to Nineveh because he knew that God is a compassionate God. To do mission in Nineveh implied trusting solely in God and not in the prejudices that distorted the popular concept of Israel's election. In other words, to do mission in Nineveh would lead Israel to modify its sense of election by recognizing its special place and responsibility in the history of salvation, rather than confusing it with exclusivity and privilege.

4. *"Remember that you were a slave in the land of Egypt...therefore the* LORD *your God commanded you."* One critical aspect of Israel's faith is the experience of the liberation from Egypt. The Pentateuch makes frequent reference to the experience of slavery in Egypt and to the people's liberation as an ethical and missional criterion for the life of the people. The memory of liberation from the yoke of slavery in Egypt proclaims that God has opted for the most needy, the poorest of the poor.

Liberation is an important theme in the history and mission of Israel. The prophets remind the people and their leaders of "God's preferential option for the poor and the oppressed." The story of God's option—with God's people in Egypt, as well as with other marginalized and exploited peoples—is commemorated in the Pentateuch, in the oracles of the prophets, in the poems of the wisdom literature, and in rituals—particularly the celebration of Passover. It is a story that is "relived" throughout history and stresses the liberating character of God and Israel's responsibility to do justice.

Israel's mission, like the church's mission, is connected to the God who declared: "I have observed the misery of my people. . . . I have heard their cry on account of their taskmasters," and therefore has come down to deliver them (Exodus 3:7-8). The character of God's mission toward God's people in Egypt, and the gift of freedom from slavery, are theological and missional criteria that proclaim who God is, what God's mission is, and how the church ought to live in the face of injustice. Therefore, the church's participation in the mission of God constitutes taking sides on behalf of the poor, becoming a voice for the voiceless, and celebrating the prophetic word of liberation and reconciliation.

5. *"Shalom."* The Hebrew Bible also makes reference to a state of life in which justice and peace govern relationships between human beings and creation. The word *shalom* implies the existence of *peace with justice*; it is the reality of an absence of violence because of the existence of justice. The prophetic passages about the Messiah's reign in the book of Isaiah present reconciling images between human beings, creation, and God. Moreover, the word *shalom* integrates the history of God's salvation with human history, eliminating dualistic attitudes that deny God's activity in our historical reality.

The biblical concept of shalom also has the potential of integrating the theology of salvation and ecology with a biblical theology of mission. Its inclusion of images of creation interacting with human beings allows the recapturing of the forgotten theme of stewardship of natural resources and the relationship of these with the survival of all creation.

6. *The cultural encounter and religious interchange between pagan peoples and Israel.* Frequently, our education and biblical tradition do not allow us to see clearly the theological and missional implications of the encounters of biblical characters—be they Israelite or Gentile—with other cultures and experiences of faith. Our interpretations are frequently formed through the model of interpretation *from the center*, due to a lack of knowledge about a particular culture or religion, to prejudice, or to the legacy of our Christian tradition concerning other cultures and religions. Therefore, too often we miss the complexity and richness of these biblical passages. Reiterating positions founded on suspicion and ignorance about persons of other cultures and faiths, we miss the opportunity to discern God's mission with these persons and peoples. The encounter of Hagar and Ishmael with God (Genesis 16; 21:8-21); the spies who received protection from Rahab, an outsider (Joshua 2); Saul's visit to the "diviner" (1 Samuel 28); and the dilemmas of Queen Esther in the court of Ahasuerus (Esther 4–6) are just a few of the biblical texts that can enrich our faith when read from the perspective of the encounter between cultures and religion.

Moreover, many biblical passages signal—implicitly or explicitly—the religious interchange that occurs when these encounters happen. There is a natural tendency in our form of reading the biblical text "not to see"—or in the worst cases, "to ignore"—this exchange of patterns of religious significance. We should now read the biblical text critically and evaluate the character of the encounters and the religious interchange.

7. *The eschatological character of mission.* There are certain texts in the Hebrew Bible, above all in Isaiah 2, that have a clearly missionary character; that is, they refer to the salvation of the nations. These texts seem to be best interpreted in an eschatological sense, for they point to the day when salvation shall reach every corner of the earth.

Within the context of the Hebrew Bible, there is not a concept of an "evangelization" of the world that has to take place through the efforts of Israel. Rather, God's salvation manifests itself in God's chosen people. This concept of "evangelization," in which the chosen people act as an instrument of God, has an eschatological character of "the last days" and will occur only by the sovereign decision of the Most High.

In the Hebrew Bible, mission is not another obligation that is laid upon Israel through all their history as part of their work as the chosen people. Rather, it is one of the signs of the eschatological times.

The New Testament and Mission

The New Testament also provides criteria and core themes for a biblical theology of mission. That which determines if the texts have a missionary nuance is not a literal reading or a traditional interpretation of the passage, but rather the *missional perspective with which the text is read.* Consequently, the passages in which Jesus encounters a foreign woman (Matthew 15:21-28; Mark 7:24-30) can be read as a "mission paradigm" with different possibilities. The gender perspective—the encounter of Jesus (a man) with a woman—is one; the interreligious perspective—the encounter of Jesus (a Jew) with a non-Jew—is another; the intercultural perspective—the encounter of Jesus (an Israelite) with a foreigner of mixed blood—is yet another.

In this section we will propose some missional criteria or views for reading the New Testament from the perspective of a biblical theology of mission. These criteria serve as core themes for reflecting about the church's mission and the Bible. In no way do these criteria exhaust the many interpretations of the New Testament, however, in my opinion, they do represent the great missionary challenges for the church of Jesus Christ in this millennium.

1. *Jesus and his ministry.* Any missional reflection about the New Testament needs to take very seriously the ministry of Jesus as presented in the Gospels. The death and resurrection of Jesus are connected with his ministry as a teacher, his announcement of the Reign of God, and with his many relationships in life: with children, women, and men; with the Jewish and Roman authorities and institutions of his society; with the fisherman, persons of other cultures, and his disciples; and with his Father.

In some Christian circles, the Jesus event has been reduced to the cross and to the benefits of salvation that come from Jesus' death. This perspective needs to be enriched by a profound study of the life and ministry of Jesus, pointing out for Christian people not only salvation, but also the significance of the incarnation of Jesus and the meaning of living out God's salvation in history; living out the Reign of God.

2. *The church: mission community in the Spirit.* It is the Holy Spirit who empowers the church for mission and discipleship. It is also the Holy Spirit who pushes and surprises the church in mission, such as happened to Peter in his encounter with Cornelius (Acts 10). Furthermore, it is the Spirit of Christ who brings about Christ's reconciliation within the community of believers, breaking down cultural, ethnic, economic, and religious walls. It is the Holy Spirit who "does mission," before our words or actions. God, in the Spirit, does mission and reveals God's grace by preparing hearts and minds for the message of Christ (Romans 1–2).

The work of the Spirit, inside as well as outside of the church, requires serious and profound thought. The Spirit works as a missional bridge, guiding the community of faith in its discernment of its mission, discipleship, and witness to the broader community and world. The Holy Spirit pulls the Christian community into new and exciting missional opportunities and challenges. This is a new theological dimension in missiological circles. The contribution of the Pentecostal tradition has been and continues to be important in the development of a theology of the Holy Spirit in the context of mission. To be a community of mission in the Spirit allows the church to live on the frontier of being a sign and agent of the mission of the kingdom of God; it confirms that the church is *an object and a subject* of the mission of God.

3. *The option for life.* The missional witness of the New Testament points to life. The ministry of Jesus does not end with death. His ministry and faithfulness to the Father give Jesus the power over death in the event of the Resurrection. All missionary activity on the part of the disciples emerges from the resurrection of the Master. The Resurrection and life mark the beginning of the church and of the new era that ends with the coming of the Kingdom.

The miracles and teachings of Jesus also point toward the concrete reality of life and the Reign of God. Jesus healed, cleaned, raised, reconciled, protected, and forgave in order that the persons he ministered to could take control of their lives, be witnesses to the good news of the Reign of God, and be free from the power of evil and sin. The teachings of Jesus, particularly the Sermon on the Mount, demonstrate the way in which one finds life in service to God and to human beings in acts of Christian solidarity.

4. *The cultural transformation of the gospel.* The New Testament is filled with examples that witness to the complex relationship between the gospel and cultures. Usually we read the New Testament texts and miss the form in which the gospel *changes* when it passes to Gentile cultural contexts. For example, while for the church in Jerusalem the title of Jesus as Messiah had a special significance, for the Gentiles it did not. It was in the Gentile context—influenced by Greek and Hellenistic philosophy—that the title of "Lord," which remains until our day, was incorporated into theology. The biblical witness of this dynamic between the gospel and cultures is of major importance in the studies of missiology, especially when we observe large cultural transformations and an enormous vitality of the Christian faith in contexts radically different from Western Christianity.

5. *The intercultural and religious encounter.* The dynamic between the gospel and cultures also points to the dynamic of the encounter between cultures and religious experiences. The Christian faith was born and developed within a context of extreme religious pluralism and intercultural encounter. The preaching of the apostles, the exhortation of Christian leaders to congregations throughout the Roman Empire, and the acts of compassion and mission of these congregations occurred in situations of constant cultural and

religious interchange. For example, how can we interpret Paul's words: "Otherwise, what will those people do who receive baptism on behalf of the dead? If the dead are not raised at all, why are people baptized on their behalf?" (1 Corinthians 15:29). Can baptism for the dead be justified with these words? Why does Paul use this example on which to base the theology of the resurrection of the body in Corinthians? Is it due to some theological, cultural, or religious significance that Paul uses this example to present his theology of the Resurrection? Questions such as these are of missional character and reflect the complexity of the encounter between cultures and religion in the New Testament.

6. *The "eschatological" factor in the New Testament and mission.* Jesus predicted the coming of the kingdom of God: "The time is fulfilled, and the kingdom of God has come near; repent, and believe in the good news" (Mark 1:15). Eschatology is the "theology of the last days"; it is the theology that reflects and helps the church of Jesus Christ live in the last days. With the insertion of Jesus in history, time is fulfilled. Therefore, we live as believers in a critical time.

God's mission, the participation of God in human history, is extraordinary even in everyday life; God's time enters the history of humanity. A biblical theology of mission has an eschatological dimension that needs to be studied. This dimension will help Christian congregations clarify the significance of living in the last days. Mission in the last days is not the denial of Christian responsibility in the world. To the contrary, the rediscovery of eschatological theology in our participation in God's mission will allow us to recapture *the relationship* of God with the world and, therefore, our *relationship* with the world.

A Contribution to the Missional Hermeneutic: Religious Pluralism, the Bible, and Mission

As we indicated earlier, the *missional hermeneutic* is a developing discipline in the field of missiology. I want, therefore, to make a concise contribution to the *missional hermeneutic* by proposing some ideas and questions that will help us discern the missional significance of the Scriptures in a context of religious pluralism.

In the first place, it is important to accept that part of Christian religious literature is (1) part of the Jewish religious literature and is (2) used by other religious groups: Jehovah's Witnesses, Mormons, Seventh Day Adventists, New Age groups, and others. For many believers, this is a scandal and cause for religious competition. For others, it is an opportunity for mission and dialogue. In any case, the use of the Scriptures is not exclusive to the Christian tradition.

The challenge of this "sharing" of the Scriptures requires primarily that the Christian community *know the Scriptures. Knowing the Scriptures* means that we know their content just as we know the content of a book of stories or an anthology of essays. Of equal importance is to know the different interpretations that enrich the understanding of the Scriptures. The work of developing a biblical theology of mission demands the accessibility and openness to diverse perspectives in biblical interpretation, from the most conservative to the most radical, from the most traditional to those that are born out of the other religious traditions that share the Scriptures.

Second, we encounter biblical characters in the sacred books of other religions, particularly those of Judaism and Islam. The images and interpretations that Jewish and Muslim communities have of these characters—Abraham, Ishmael, Sarah, Hagar, Mary the mother of Jesus, and Jesus, among others—are an invitation to reconsider and reread our interpretations with new lenses and perspectives. Formed under the model of biblical interpretation *from the center*, it is common to reject this type of missional reading. However, this encounter between sacred texts offers the possibility of increasing our biblical understanding and enriching our interpretations of these texts.

Third, there are religious traditions and persons of agnostic belief that have a profound respect for our Lord, Jesus Christ. The life and ministry of Jesus appeal to persons who search for models for living with human integrity and a sense of justice. For example, a substantial number of "investigators" of Christianity in China feel deeply attracted to the figure of Jesus. Some of these investigators consider themselves "cultural Christians," a phrase that implies a certain sympathy for the Christian faith. This sense of respect for the figure of Jesus in persons of other faiths or ideological positions can be turned into an opportunity for dialogue and mission. Their interpretations of the Scriptures can enrich our interpretation and understanding of the Bible.

Fourth, there is an enormous spiritual richness in reading and sharing the Scriptures with persons of other religions. I know of a missionary in Taiwan who learned Mandarin (Chinese) from a Buddhist tutor. The tutor used the Bible to teach the language. The educational process allowed the missionary *to know* the Scriptures through a Buddhist lens, and her experience of faith was enriched enormously. In addition, the Buddhist tutor has begun *to know* the Christian Scriptures and continues to use them in the spiritual practices of her tradition.

A biblical theology of mission ought to utilize all the resources of biblical interpretation that are available, including methods and models of interpretation and interpretations that other religious traditions offer. In the work of developing a biblical theology of mission, the Christian community is responsible for discovering the richness of our biblical tradition. Providentially, this richness is not confined to the interpretation of the Christian community. Quite the contrary is true, for God's self-disclosure in the Christian Scriptures, just as in Jesus Christ, is open to be discovered by all.

The *missional hermeneutic* needs, therefore, to share with the world the questions: (1) Why mission? (2) How is mission done? and (3) What is mission? In the process of listening to diverse answers to these missional questions, the church discovers the activity of God in particular contexts, the work of the Spirit of Christ in the world. Upon adding other voices to our *missional hermeneutic* we allow the God of mission to mark the path of God's mission for the church of Jesus Christ.

These new voices in our *missional hermeneutic* disrupt the metaphor of the missional tapestry described earlier. Now we have God's missionary activity in the world—vertical threads—the response of the people of God to this missionary activity—horizontal threads—and the voices of the world—*the context of God's missionary activity!* How can these voices of the world be included in our participation in God's mission?

My uncle Eugenio was a fisherman in Puerto Rico. One of his many responsibilities was making fishing nets, and to this art he dedicated long hours. His ability to make knots that unite vertical and horizontal threads and create a net was impressive. Once the net is finished, the knots join the threads from all directions. The knots are converted into the central points where the horizontal, vertical, and diagonal threads are joined. These knots can sustain the weight of the fish and the fisherman's pull while raising the net to the surface. All the threads, whatever their direction, make up the knots that sustain the fish. In the same way, the *missional hermeneutic* that includes the context of God's missionary activity— the world—allows the biblical text to serve as a knot of the net, a central point that unites different directions of God's mission in the world. This *missional hermeneutic* becomes the connecting knot that sustains the pressure and the pull of God and the world. However, just as my uncle Eugenio had to put dedication and work into his net, our biblical reflection and interpretation for mission also need dedication, work, and healthy critical reflection to develop a relevant and renewing biblical theology of mission.

In the next chapter—chapter 4—we shall study different theologies of mission that have developed during the twentieth century. These theologies of mission are formulated primarily by missiologists in the West, though not exclusively. We will also point to some of the new perspectives in mission theology, particularly emerging as a result of the voice of the Fourth-Fifths World missiologists and theologians. Many of these theologies reflect the implications and consequences of mission that we discussed in the first chapter, and the tensions that occur as missiologists and theologians continue to develop new perspectives in their thought and practice.

---

1. Robert Schreiter, "The Bible and Mission: A Response to Walter Brueggemann and Beverly Gaventa," *Missiology* 10.4 (October 1982): 431; for further discussion see pages 431-34.

CHAPTER FOUR

Mission and Church, Gospel and World

Mission Theologies for Today— and Perhaps for Tomorrow

In this chapter we shall study some of the most important theologies of mission during the twentieth century. These theologies, in my opinion, will continue to serve the global Christian community well into the twenty-first century. Some of them will continue to grow and evolve; they will thrive in the context of a postmodern world. Others may slowly lose momentum in this same context, giving an impression of running their course. Yet others will continue to create debates and controversies, demonstrating the many perspectives in the Christian global family. All of them, however, do not have a life of their own nor do they emerge out of thin air. Theologies of mission—just as any theology—are grounded in the praxis of the Christian community around the world. Good theology, as world Christianity scholar Andrew Walls has argued, is born where the Christian faith has vitality. There is, consequently, a correlation between good theology, good missiology, and the vitality of the Christian faith.

Before we begin our presentation and discussion of these mission theologies, I need to provide the reader with four guiding metaphors that exemplify different reference points in mission thought and practice. These metaphors illustrate the core understanding of mission theologies and practice in a particular time and context. Though different, they are related. Their relationship is not based on progression and accumulation of mission knowledge and experience. It is not a ladder-type structure where the first step is primitive and every other step upward means improvement. The relationship between these metaphors is based on a *continuum*: they all share and flow in the same history, they coexist and overlap one another, they nourish and shape one another, and they witness to the life of Christian communities as they struggle to discern and participate in the building of God's Reign. These metaphors also provide an image that projects the missiological relationship between Christian churches, their mission, and the world.

Metaphors for Church, Gospel, Mission and the World

The Church as the *Rescue Boat for the World*

In the mid–nineteenth and early twentieth centuries, the Protestant missionary movement was debating the relationship between mission and the church. Previously, the main agent in mission practice and theology had been mission agencies or societies, such as the London Missionary Society, the Board of Commissioners, and others. Some of these boards, such as the Woman's Foreign Missionary Society and the Missionary Society of Argentina, Brazil, and Liberia, were sponsored by denominations and kept a close relationship with church bodies. However, this relationship continued to foster a gap between mission practice, theology, and church life.

Mission work was to be administered, programmed, and evaluated by the societies and boards. While societies and boards provided reports to denominations and church bodies, the latter informed congregations with the frequent, but unfortunate fractional impact that these reports usually have on local church life. The relationship between mission and church continued to be mediated by these organizations, creating an institutional pattern and structure that separated church life and mission until the mid–twentieth century. Some churches in the local and denominational spheres, though sponsoring mission boards, were not at the forefront of mission work, or integrating mission work to their day-to-day life, but rather were focusing primarily on providing resources, both material and human, for the mission agencies.

Interestingly, the separation between church and mission was evident in that many of the young people who became missionaries under many of these societies in the late 1800s and early 1900s also received their vocation for mission in conferences and events sponsored and funded by these societies. Certainly there were cases where local congregations played an important role in helping young people define their mission vocation. Nevertheless, it was the students' Christian movements, such as the Student Volunteer movement and the World Student Christian Federation, strongly affiliated to mission societies and boards, who provided the "sacred space" for initiating and fostering the mission vocations during this period.

As early as 1910, at the World Mission Conference at Edinburgh, the Conference began to explore, though implicitly, what had been in the minds of many missional leaders: the critical relationship between the church and mission. During the next decades, the world missionary movement, celebrating different regional and world conferences, focused on this missiological concern and slowly discovered the centrality of the church in mission work. The church was no longer in the background of mission work, but was rather the agent of mission, a mission agency, a community that proclaimed in word and deed the good news of the gospel of Jesus Christ.

With this emerging awareness, did mission agencies disappear? No, they did not. However, their approach to recruitment, their search for support, and their relationship with Christian churches and denominations has changed, recognizing in the church an institution with a missionary mandate and character committed to support and uphold missionary endeavors, particularly overseas.

In the United States, there continues to be an ambiguous relationship between mission agencies—which continue to promote missionary work on a volunteer basis—congregations, and denominational mission boards. It is evident that the missiological reflection of the first half of the twentieth century did not resolve the misson agencies/church-based dilemma inherited from nineteenth- and early-twentieth-centuries mission practice and theology. Nevertheless, there was a shift in the theological outlook of mission work, and the church came to be a critical focal point in the practice and theology of mission.

As the relationship between mission and church gained grounding in the world missionary movement, a particular self-understanding of the church-in-mission emerged. This self-understanding developed into an ecclesiocentric mode of doing and reflecting on mission: the church became *a saving boat for the world*. This meant that the church knew and had the gospel, and was the herald of the true gospel to the world. The church was to rescue the world from (1) the forces of secularization and unjust industrialization around the world; (2) the extreme poverty and underdevelopment of the non-Christian world (Africa, Asia, Latin America); and (3) the deficiency and inadequacy of other religions to face the challenges of the modern and progressive world. The urgent task of the church was both proclaiming the gospel to all people awaiting the imminent Second Coming of Christ and civilizing all the people in order to establish the kingdom of God on earth. The latter was a historical and progressive understanding of the Kingdom promoted by liberal minds called the Social Gospel, which influenced missional circles and came to a crisis as a result of the two world wars. Hence, the church became the *mission agent par excellence*, establishing the criterion for the communication and the appropriate reception of the gospel, church life, and church and societal order.

In 1948, the ecumenical movement, particularly its expression in the World Council of Churches (WCC), incorporated into its structures the International Missionary Council (IMC) and named it the Commission for Evangelization and Mission of the WCC. The IMC, a direct result of the World Missionary Conference at Edinburgh in 1910, was an ecumenical organization made up of national Christian councils and missionary societies from throughout the world that dealt with diverse missional issues—strategies, theologies, cooperation—and coordinated the World Missionary Conferences until that year. This incorporation, though received with many reservations from some evangelical missionary groups, crystallized and further developed the missional practice and reflection of the time: church and mission were two sides of the same coin.

This metaphor should not be misinterpreted. For example, as early as the first decades of the twentieth century, some missiologists engaged in interreligious dialogue with people of other faiths. The dialogue recognized the integrity of other faiths, their contribution to an understanding about God and God's purposes for creation, and their spirituality as a source for relating to God. However, with very few exceptions, most of these missiologists concluded that these faiths lacked the "completeness" of the Christian faith and the institutional medium, the church, for the proper practice of the faith. Being the *rescue boat for the world* or the *mission agent par excellence* did not mean that the Christian missionary endeavor—ecclesiocentric in nature—was always blind and dismissive of important religious and social issues in its mission context. On the contrary, many were very aware of their context. The difference is that most of the endeavors faced the contextual issues with a prepared, *a priori* answer: come join the church, for we have and are the *only* answer to your problems.

Before I move to the next metaphor, it is important for the reader to recognize that the church as a *rescue boat for the world* has a strong affinity with and support of the colonial periods of the late–nineteenth and early twentieth centuries. The geographic extension of the empires served, in many occasions, the missionary endeavors overseas. It is true that at times the empires had problems with the missionary presence, which at times named the injustices and oppression of the empires' politics, but the political and cultural ethos represented by the missionary presence supported even the most subtle racism and classism. Colonialism, and later neocolonialism, was a force that many missionaries reckoned with, but also one that provided the cultural foundation for a too frequent racist missiology that still needs to be abolished. Once more we can see how our own context, our own social, political, economic, and cultural contours shape our self-understanding and practice of mission. If we come from a society that practices racism and classism, we will certainly find in our self-understanding of the gospel and mission work levels of these social illnesses; this is the negative side of communicating a contextualized gospel and the need to understand ourselves, as God's missionary people, as objects of God's mission.

Roman Catholic and early Pentecostal mission endeavors also shared this self-understanding of mission practice and theology until well into the twentieth century. With some exceptions, the main theological thrust continued to be ecclesiocentric, the church as a *rescue boat for the world*. As I will discuss below, the Roman Catholic Church will enter a new understanding of mission after

75

the Second Vatican Council, while the Protestant and Pentecostal traditions will continue to struggle with this legacy as they search for new ways of being faithful to God's mission.

The Church as a *Sign of the Reign of God*

The study of the New Testament and the challenges in mission practice and theology late in the 1950s brought into serious question the metaphor of the church as a *rescue boat for the world*. In the world missionary and ecumenical movements, the voice of J. Hoekendijk, a Dutch missiologist who actively participated in the International Missionary Council, and the author of *The Church Inside Out*, strongly argued against the ecclesiocentric mission trend and proposed a shift toward the centrality and activity of God in mission work. Progressively, Hoekendijk's work contributed to the *missio Dei* metaphor, which was discussed in chapter 2 and which I will discuss further in this chapter. However, after catastrophic events in the "Christian world," such as the two world wars, Christian missiologists developed a suspicion toward the church as the institution of mission agency, and searched for biblical and theological resources that would provide a stronger and broader missiological framework to reflect and act in faithfulness to God's missionary calling. Hoekendijk and others were critical of the church and wanted to relativize the church's self-understanding in mission work, but were not willing to dispense with the church.

Early in the 1960s, the Roman Catholic Church and Pope John XXIII convened the Second Vatican Council. The Council, a serious engagement with and for the *aggiornamento* (meaning updating, to become relevant and responsive to the present day) of the church, provided a rich but different understanding of mission and of the church's participation in mission. Almost simultaneously, the missionary and ecumenical movements were appropriating the "Reign of God" theme to do and evaluate their mission practice and theology.

With the Reign of God mission theme, the world continues to be the object of mission. The church, on the one hand, is not the Reign of God on earth, displacing the ecclesiocentric trend, but *a sign* of the Reign of God on earth. The gospel to be incarnated, on the other hand, is the gospel preached and lived by Jesus Christ in the four

Gospels: the good news of the Reign of God. The relationship of the church with the world is an eschatological one. The church, as Second Vatican Council declares, is God's sacrament for the world. The church is, therefore, a medium of salvation, an expression of God's will for God's people and creation, and a witness of God's divine will for all creation.

God's mission in the world is bringing the Reign to its fulfillment. The church's mission, as stated above, is to be a sign of this fulfillment for humankind and creation. At times the language used to describe the mission of the church referred to the church's participation in bringing the Reign of God to fulfillment. Notice, however, the secondary location of the church's missionary activity: the church is not the Reign of God nor is it the agent of the Reign of God. The church is merely *a sign* of the Reign of God.

This new self-understanding of the church's role in mission was also the result of the growing voices of the non-Western Christian churches, particularly Protestant and Orthodox, in the missionary and ecumenical movements. It was also a time of emancipation from old colonial models, though a new form of colonialism—neo-colonialism—characterized by economic dependency, continued to oppress underdeveloped nations in the southern and eastern regions.

In the Roman Catholic Church this non-Western voice was crucial given that Pope John XXIII had appointed the most diverse and international council in the church's history. Among evangelical groups, particularly those associated with what is known today as the Lausanne movement, the non-Western voice was heard in evangelical missiologists such as Orlando Costas and others who "rocked the boat" of well-established ecclesiocentric and Western missional foundations. It was evident that the voices of those evangelized and missionized people had a different vision and expected a different practice and theology of mission for their own and other contexts.

Theologically, the church as a sign of the Reign of God found in Jesus' ministry an important model for mission practice and theology. For a significant time, many Christian communities took the motto "Mission in Christ's Way" to reflect and engage in mission activity, whether overseas or domestic. The Lord's Prayer, a synthesis of Jesus' mission focusing on the centrality of God's activity in the world, was studied in the missionary and ecumenical movements and became a fresh, but at times controversial, missionary proposal. It was clear that the missiological shift had gone from an ecclesiocentric approach, to a theocentric, Reign-of-God-driven theology of mission.

Did these changes ever touch local congregations? Did mission theologies and practices change in Christian congregations? I believe that to a certain extent congregations, whether Roman Catholic, Protestant, Pentecostal, or Orthodox, have gained a new language and perspective. Even if they might have an ecclesiocentric view of mission, this view was challenged by other proposals such as the one described above. It is difficult to evaluate the level of awareness and integration of these missiological changes. There are so many factors that either contribute or impede a Christian community to be up-to-date in mission theologies and practices. Moreover, though many acquired the new language—Reign of God, mission in Christ's way, and so forth—many continue to be confused and ambiguous, in captivity (see chapter 1), to their practices and theologies of mission.

The Church in the *Matrix of Mission:*
The Trinity and *Missio Dei*

In chapter 1, I provided and discussed a definition of mission. In this definition I emphasized the relational character of the Trinity, the Christian community, the world, and Christian mission. Though the metaphor of the Reign of God is theocentric and eschatological, it does not carry the *dynamo*, the relational momentum, the movement that mission requires.

As I stated in chapter 1, it is evident that the New Testament gives witness to the mutual relationship of the community of the Triune God—God the Creator, God the Redeemer, and God the Sustainer—in mission. In *missio Dei,* God is the primordial agent of and in mission; mission is thus an *event in and of community.* God's mission is a participatory and communal activity among Godself. God the Creator sends God the Redeemer, and God the Redeemer sends God the Sustainer and the church. In this "sending" the church is never found absent of God's missional activity, but rather accompanied, guided, and in community with and by the Spirit of Christ in the church's discernment and coparticipation in mission.

78

This communal participation in mission is uniquely cross-cultural. The missional purposes of the Triune God—one God, three persons—become real through the activity of three different expressions of God. It is this interplaying relationship of the three persons of the Trinity and Christian communities that provides a new understanding of mission. This communal and mutually dependent character of the Triune God is described with the Greek term *perichoresis*. This *perichoretic*, interdependent relationship between the Triune God and God's people in mission is what I call the *matrix of mission*.

The church, as a community in mission, is in the *matrix of mission*. Thus, the church is not only a subject of mission—which by itself renders into an ecclesiocentric practice of mission—but it is also an object of mission, completely "covered," "embraced" in God's missionary activity, called to repent, change, and renew its missionary commitment and practice in the world. Through God's missionary activity in the world, Christian communities coparticipating in God's mission learn to *live* the gospel of the Reign of God, hence, begin to understand it. The gospel is more than propositional statements about doctrine and order. The gospel is God's living action of redemption and liberation for creation. The gospel is alive and has movement in the world. It is the force that resists evil and transforms death into life. It is the gift and hope of reconciliation despite war and injustice. It is the power of liberation in a world of oppression. Thus, the eschatological dimension in the *matrix of mission* is found in the confrontation between God's liberating power and the oppressive and destructive powers of evil in this world. The Christian community, when living the gospel of Jesus Christ, is participating in God's mission and experiencing "the end times," the eschatological moments that point to God's continuing work in the cosmos.

What can we gather from these metaphors in relation to the church's self-understanding of its role in mission? First, the self-understanding of the church's role in mission has changed with time. Different historical forces, such as the world missionary movement, the colonial and neocolonial period, the emerging voices of Christians in "missionary lands," and the vitality of the faith in non-Christian lands, proved to be a catalyst to broaden the missional reflection. Second, one metaphor, one perspective, is not enough to understand the complex but intriguing relationship between the church, mission, and the world. Third, though one metaphor or perspective is not enough, we must recognize that there are metaphors more comprehensive than others. It is evident that the missiological reflection on the theologies and practices of mission in relation to the church has been enriched by a more global, critical, prophetic participation of the people of God, particularly those at the margins who are often the focus of mission. Fourth, the movement in these metaphors shows a theocentric, Reign-of-God, Trinitarian basis in mission, rather than an ecclesiocentric, church-is-Kingdom perspective. This movement includes the people of God as both recipients and agents in mission, learners and doers, objects and subjects of God's mission.

Metaphors are sources to help us understand our complex reality as God's people in mission. The above metaphors demonstrate the vitality of Christian mission. These metaphors carry their own limitations and problems. They also show the multiple theological themes that shape the discipline of missiology. All of these metaphors attempt to give a sound theological response to the relationship between mission, church, gospel, and world. As stated above, some metaphors are stronger, tighter than others. Yet, all of them, though contextual and contingent, are expressions of dilemmas found in discerning and assessing the church's participation and understanding of God's missionary activity.

Mission Theologies Today— and Perhaps for Tomorrow

In the last section of his book *Transforming Mission*, David Bosch provides what he calls the "ecumenical paradigm of mission." He discusses at length some of the critical changes in mission theology and practice, identifying thirteen different starting points in mission. Using the rubric of *mission as* (for example, *contextualization, evangelization, liberation,* and others), he critically describes, explains, and evaluates some of the new (and old) mission practices and theologies. In this section I will synthesize some of his work, although I will use a different scheme and will provide my own interpretation of some of his work.

Mission is about transmission and reception of the gospel. On the transmission side, the issues are frequently focused on the missionary activity, the one who goes and does. Some of the questions related to the transmitting task are: What are we to communicate as the gospel? How do we participate in mission among people of different cultures, with different histories, with different faiths, and so on? Are we to help bring justice? How does our economic background shape our mission practice and the way people perceive who we are as Christians?

On the reception side, the issues are frequently focused on the activity of those who are missionized. Some questions related to the reception side are: As missionized people, what do we do with the gospel received? Can we understand it as it was received? Is this gospel an agent for our well-being? How is this gospel related to our non-Christian context, history, and family relationships? How will this gospel be part of our history as a particular people?

Using these two dimensions of mission, the transmission and reception process, I will discuss what I consider to be some of the most important mission theologies and practices for today—and perhaps for tomorrow.

Mission as Transmission

1. *Mission as evangelization* continues to be an important task in the life of Christian communities. Evangelization is the process by which the gospel is communicated, understood, lived, and integrated into the life of a community. Evangelization, consequently, is not only about proclamation, but it is also about discipleship: living the gift of salvation in Jesus Christ by growing, maturing, and witnessing in and to the gospel of Christ.

Many Christian communities continue to separate evangelization from social justice. This separation frequently comes from a superficial understanding of evangelization, for true evangelization will lead us into actions that give witness to the gospel—one being our acts of justice on behalf of those suffering injustice. This is an intrinsic part of what it means to be a disciple of Christ, one who lives the gospel in all the levels of life.

Evangelization is also about communication and spiritual insight. Recently, I was invited to give a workshop on evangelization. I was given the topic, "When fear does not let us share the gospel." As I began the workshop, it was clear that many in the workshop had complaints about the hostile environment when sharing the gospel in their community. They could not find ways to introduce the gospel without being uncomfortable or concerned about imposing their religion.

Regrettably, part of the misunderstanding of evangelization is the assumed starting point: to give answers. We have rarely thought about another approach, another starting point: the religious practice (or religiosity) of those whom we are called to evangelize. If God's missionary activity is in the world, then we do not need to begin with answers from scratch. We begin by discerning what God has been doing among those in our communities. We will find in our search different responses: from blunt denial of God's invitation to salvation and relationship, to resistance, to sympathetic affinity, to waiting for further clarification and dialogue about God's invitation. The process of evangelization demands a different approach to communicate the gospel. It also demands a different understanding of conversion, of the experience by which a person turns to God, through Jesus Christ and the power of the Holy Spirit. Turning to God is a process; it requires time and a trusting relationship in order to go beyond informing about Christ to forming in Christ, becoming part of the Christian community. It is a process by which the experience of and with God becomes *humanized*; the gift of salvation becomes historical, affectionate, relational, and grounded in living the gospel of Jesus Christ within community.

2. *Mission as the church-with-others* is a missional expression of solidarity and accompaniment with Christian people, people of other faiths, and/or with nonreligious communities. *Mission as the church-with-others* celebrates the mystery of Christian presence, the sacramental act of solidarity in times of need and support. In its sacramental act, the church discovers and is nourished by God's activity in others. These are times when frequently the church says: "We went to give, and yet we have received."

Mission as the church-with-others requires the Christian community to acknowledge God's missional activity with those to be served. It also requires the church to take a risk, to accept others' interpretation of life and struggle as true and unique. The church also needs to be a learner as it practices solidarity and accompaniment, as it serves the needs of others, as it learns about human limitations and God's grace, about resisting evil, about hope, about sin—both personal and in societal structures—and liberation, about hate and reconciliation. In this mission practice our mission theology is enhanced, broadened, and transformed.

Mission as the church-with-others is celebratory and prophetic. Just as the church celebrates God's mission and the church's learnings with the others, in its witness of solidarity and accompaniment, the church embodies the justice of the gospel of Jesus Christ. In the celebratory spirit of community and sacramental activity, the church becomes an agent of evangelization, giving glory to God and announcing the Reign of God. The ultimate reason for our solidarity is based on God's purpose for the world, the coming of the Reign of God.

Mission as the church-with-others is also an expression of *mission as common witness.* As congregations and denominations join together to give witness to the Reign of God, the Christian community proclaims and discovers God's gift of unity to the church catholic. Mission is an expression of God's grace and redemption beyond the boundaries of denominational order and discipline.

3. *Mission as witness to people of other faiths* is one of the most challenging dimensions of mission theology and practice. Due to secularization, many philosophers and theologians expected the decline of religions and religious effervescence. Ironically, religious consciousness and practice have not disappeared, but have been transformed. Christian communities face a complex and diverse religious map, one that is pregnant with opportunities and hostilities.

Theologians have posed three different theological and missional categories to describe the way in which Christianity relates to other faiths. The first one is the exclusivist category. In this category, Christians claim the uniqueness of their faith and recognize no salvation in other faiths. The second is the inclusivist category, which is generally associated with Karl Rahner's *anonymous Christianity.* This perspective refers to God's saving grace in all religions that seek for the good. The inclusivist category recognizes the more or less legitimate means of salvation in other faiths, though they are legitimate means of salvation because of Christ's saving grace in them. The third category is the pluralist category. This category recognizes that all faiths are legitimate means of salvation.

Mission as witness to people of other faiths poses critical questions regarding salvation, the role of the church, God's presence in other people's faith, the work of the Holy Spirit, the Trinity, dialogue, history, and inculturation—another mission category to be discussed in the next section. This is a missional area that on the one hand carries many prejudices and misconceptions inherited from Christendom. On the other, there is rich historical and theological material that wrestles with these issues, and yet many involved in this endeavor have little or inadequate knowledge of these contributions. Furthermore, *mission as witness to people of other faiths* is a missiological endeavor with no guarantees, overwhelmed with uncertainties, and requiring deep commitment despite possible frustrations *and* achievements. It is truly a missional task dependent on prayer, open to new venues of understanding God's grace and work, and demanding a strong Christian commitment with a deep hunger for God's mystery in people of other faiths.

Mission as Reception

4. *Mission as liberation* is a Christian response to the oppressive economic and political structures of evil in this world. Liberation theology, born in Latin America, continues to have an impressive influence on both the practice and theology of mission. As stated in previous chapters, Evangelicals and Pentecostals, particularly those living in the Four-Fifths World, have also appropriated liberation commitments, prophetic convictions, and theological perspectives as they do mission among the poorest of the poor.

Mission as liberation recognizes that the gospel has a *preferential option for the poor*, as discussed in chapter 2. The poor of the earth have a unique perspective on liberation, since their social and ideological location has no economic interest. The poor then are able to "read" the ideological inclinations of those in positions of wealth and power. They are able to name society's idolatrous practices and rhetoric, providing a prophetic voice calling for repentance and solidarity and seeking social transformation.

In this mission practice and theology, the agent of liberation is God and the poor. The poor are the subjects of their history and struggle, accompanied by the God of liberation. Whereas other models of mission, for instance mission as justice (not discussed in this section, but discussed at length in David Bosch's book *Transforming Mission*), seek to bring about justice from the top, seeking reformation in the upper power structures in the broader system, *mission as liberation* begins with the needs and the voice of the poor. This does not mean that this mission practice dismisses dialogue with the economic and political powers in this new global configuration. It does, however, recognize that dialogue in the upper levels of power have limited results. The agents of *mission as liberation* are well aware of the political space and strategies needed to incite change on behalf of the poor.

Mission as liberation also seeks for the liberation of those captive to the idols of wealth and affluence. It is the preferential perspective of the poor that provides a prophetic word confronting the wealthy with false ideologies (such as hard work creates money), naming for the rich their idolatrous relationship with wealth, relating the condition of the poor with the wealth of the rich, and inviting the powerful and rich to a new relationship with God that will liberate creation.

Finally, agents of *mission as liberation* also address the plight of the middle class, reminding them of their function as accomplices in further exploitation of the poor. As middle-class and upper-middle-class people continue to uphold the ideology of the powerful, the perspective of the poor gives an alternative vision of true liberation and well-being.

5. *Mission as reconciliation* seeks to heal the wounds of those involved in ethnic wars, racial oppression, gender exploitation, and any kind of injustice and violence that harm human communities and/or the environment. During the last decade, the world has witnessed an increase in violent acts against minority groups, women, children, and any other marginal group who claims a right to exist and participate in society. As nation-states lose control over borders and territory, ethnic and religious groups claim their identity while old feuds are fueled with devastating results for the most vulnerable in these groups, namely women and children. The concern for ethnic wars has become so important for governments that political scientist Samuel Huntington wrote a now famous article entitled "The Clash of Civilizations," which poses a theoretical scheme to help nation-states understand and face the problem.

In *mission as reconciliation,* the Christian community seeks justice, since reconciliation without justice is not true reconciliation. Robert Schreiter's book *Reconciliation* provides a biblical and theological framework to engage in the practice of reconciliation. In his framework, Schreiter clearly states that the victim, not the oppressor, initiates reconciliation. As a result, *mission as reconciliation* locates the

Christian community on behalf of the victims, seeking for justice in order to experience true biblical and historical reconciliation. An interesting example of this reconciling process was witnessed in the Reconciliation Commission in South Africa, chaired by Archbishop Desmund Tutu.

The human community also needs to be reconciled with its environment. Modernity has infused us with a "conquering and dominating" spirit that has jeopardized our relationship with the environment. Today the global community faces environmental deterioration. It is evident that human kind in many ways has abused creation. *Mission as reconciliation* seeks for justice between the human community and the environment, recognizing that both are in need of redemption with their Creator and in need of balance between each other.

6. *Mission as contextualization* seeks the gospel to be relevant in the context where it is transmitted. Under this missional agency, I want to discuss two other types of mission practice and theology: *mission as inculturation* and *mission as theology*. In *mission as inculturation* the Christian faith begins to grow roots in the context where the Christian community is born. Consequently, there is an interplay between the culture of the context and the community's interpretation of the received gospel. Frequently, this interplay is not intentional, but rather it flows as the people of God live their faith *in* their cultural context. The faith is incarnated, though the faith's inculturation does not always mean an easy and uncritical appropriation of particular cultural imagination and practices.

Mission as inculturation happens as the Christian community uses its own vernacular, its cultural resources, its history, its religious worldview, its present dilemmas and challenges to interpret and communicate the meaning of the gospel in its context. *Mission as inculturation* is, therefore, a process of reception to be tested in the process of transmission of the gospel in its own context. To communicate or transmit the gospel without a level of inculturation will result in communicating the good news in an incomprehensible language.

Mission as inculturation points to the never-ending power of the Holy Spirit in the process by which the receptor community appropriates the gospel. Although many historians, theologians, and congregations dismiss mission on the basis of its overwhelming imperialistic overtones, Lamin Sanneh, among other historians and missiologists, has reminded us of the more locally based mission work where emerging Christian communities inculturate the gospel in ways in which their cultural practices are reaffirmed and colonial oppression resisted. *Mission as inculturation*, therefore, is an instrument by which Christian communities take control of the meaning of the gospel in their lives, providing the broader community with an interpretation, from the underside, of the history of transmission and reception in a particular space and time.

Mission as inculturation implies that the gospel begins to have a particular cultural taste, one that is grounded within the people's context. The gospel, incarnated, for instance, in a Jamaican community, goes through a "Jamaicanization" process. One critical issue in *mission as inculturation* is, *How far should the inculturation process go?* Does the "Jamaicanization" of the gospel erode the cutting edge of the gospel, the prophetic character of the gospel for that culture? This question takes us to the second mission practice and theology I want to discuss: *mission as theology.*

Mission as theology reminds us that the theological task is always contextual. There are no such things as universal theologies—usually understood as Western theologies—or contextual theologies—usually understood as African American, womanist, feminist, and Asian theologies, among others. All theologies are contextual, therefore, in conversations are equals. *Mission as theology* also seeks to recover in the practice of mission a critical engagement with the best intellectual resources of our Christian tradition and the secular academic world. *Mission as theology* demands all the possible tools for discerning and coparticipating in God's missionary activity, including those tools from Christian spiritual disciplines. As a result, *mission as theology* resists the "if it works and God calls you, do it" mentality that has characterized in many occasions the missionary work from the United States. Furthermore, *mission as theology* is also the resource for the Christian community to explore and evaluate the inculturation process.

Mission as theology also addresses the classic theological discipline. It poses that good theology is contextual theology, since it is grounded on the life of Christian communities living their faith in the world. Theology for the sake of pure intellectual exercise has run its course. Theologies that are limited to a few who are prepared for such an enterprise and that reify or overobjectify a Christ experience (as William R. Burrows suggests in his article "A

Seventh Paradigm? Catholics and Radical Inculturation" in *Mission in Bold Humility*) are no longer valid. Good mission theology, hence, good theology, emerges out of the contexts where the Christian faith has vitality. Its vocation is not only to uphold the integrity of the gospel in the process of inculturation, but also to accompany the people of God as they discern and coparticipate in God's awesome and surprising mission.

How do some of these mission theologies take flesh in a congregation? How do they help a congregation mature in its practice and theology of mission? Mission practice and theology are always cross-cultural. Local congregations, mission agencies, and Christian denominations in North America are involved in cross-cultural mission, whether overseas or domestic. The next chapter provides theological and practical insights to engage in cross-cultural mission and see how some of these mission practices and theologies take flesh in church life.

CHAPTER FIVE

Mission as *Walking the Tightrope*

Mission as an Encounter Between Cultures

Mission is also about cultural encounters, about the interplay between cultures, and cultural encounters are about relationships. Mission history can be written using cultural encounters as a category. Mission theology should be done using thick intercultural theory. Regrettably, this awareness is just beginning to emerge in North Atlantic missiological circles as Christianity in the eastern/southern regions engages in missiological discourse providing depth and new perspectives on known issues.

Missiology is intrinsically cross-cultural. The relationship between the gospel and cultures is a critical dimension for developing theologies and strategies of mission. The diagrams (in the appendix) are a tool that can be used to understand the complex dynamics in the transmission and reception of the gospel between cultures.

These diagrams depict mission in cross-cultural encounters, the complex encounter of cultures in the midst of the *missio Dei*, or God's missionary activity. In a unique way, cultures, whether in A or in B (refer to the diagrams in the appendix), play a crucial role in the transmission and reception of the gospel. Notice how the reception of the gospel is as important as the transmission of the gospel in the matrix of mission!

Emerging from the Hispanic/Latino experience of being

evangelized and evangelizing, I want to propose the image of *walking a tightrope* to reflect on the mission activity, which entails a process of transmission, reception, and communication of the gospel—the matrix of mission. The image of *walking a tightrope* allows our missiological reflection to consider the *complex cross-cultural dynamic characterized by asymmetric encounters and interchanges between cultures*. It also allows our missiological reflection to see the activity of God, even in spaces that we might not consider missional.

We need to be increasingly aware of the asymmetry in cross-cultural encounters. I also hope that this historical and intercultural awareness may contribute to changing missional practices that have been considered imperialistic, oppressive, paternalistic, and culturally insensitive. I argue that it is precisely the lack of awareness of this complex cross-cultural dynamic, characterized by asymmetric intercultural encounters, which contributes to the confusion between unacceptable mission practices and mission renewal. In other words, I am inviting the reader to revisit the church's understandings of mission and to use her or his imagination and rationality, guided by the Spirit of Christ, to put into practice these new missiological insights in the context of our congregations. The invitation is to *walk the tightrope,* to take the risk of engaging in mission, and discover fresh missiological perspectives through our reflection and practice of mission.

Biblical Insights into Cross-Cultural Mission

The Cornelius and Peter narrative in Acts 10 provides a model for thinking about cross-cultural mission practice and theology. The text clearly presents an insider/outsider situation. It is the Holy Spirit, through visions and unprecedented actions, who initiates the possibility for a missional cross-cultural encounter.

Risks of faith and identity are needed in order to engage in cross-cultural mission. On the Cornelius side is the risk of accepting the vision of the Spirit. It is the risk of requesting the presence of somebody who Cornelius knows will not come willingly to his household. It is the risk of being humiliated, of being told "you do not have any part or doing in who we are or what we believe"; a risk of being dismissed, ignored, rejected. It is the risk of *walking the tightrope.*

On Peter's side is the risk of moving against his own cultural and political identity. It is also a risk of sharing his faith with a community that may adulterate the integrity of the belief, allowing the faith to go beyond its secure ethnic/racial/religious birthplace. It is also a risk because Peter is on the most fragile side of the encounter, since he is on the lower end of the power configuration. The asymmetrical conditions are against Peter and his community, who have suffered persecution and are in the constant threat of death.

Moreover, this text presents one of the most critical asymmetrical conditions of the time: the primal sentiment of violence between different groups. Both Cornelius and Peter represent a clash of civilizations. The Holy Spirit is pushing two persons, two representatives of different groups of people, to dwell with each other even though these cultures' social configuration hold the real possibility of violent conflict.

In spite of the above, I would like to point out that Cornelius has the clearest vision. The outsider, the one to be missionized, clearly sees God's action in his life and community. He has no hesitation or reluctance. He acts on his vision. Peter, on the other hand, struggles to understand the meaning of the unclean animals, and reckons with God's mysterious missional proposal: "Get up, Peter, kill and eat." Even when God explains, Peter is still puzzled, seeking and thinking about what this vision means.

As the story develops, the asymmetrical condition of the encounter is confusing. Should not Peter have the clear vision given his status as Jesus' disciple? Should not Cornelius, the seeker of the faith, do more in his search for God to further his faith? I believe a possible answer to these confusing asymmetrical conditions in the story is found in the encounter itself, in the cross-cultural missional process, the matrix of mission. The process provides for the encounter between both communities and is always open to the dynamics of both religious and cultural identities, without giving one hint of the outcome. It is an *open* process where histories, cultural identities, religious longings and convictions collide, and yet the Spirit never hints to any of the participants what the final and concluding situation is. It is a process where on the one hand, the force of primal intercultural violence is potentially explosive, and on the other, the force of the Spirit struggles to bond these communities in Christ despite the fears and uncertainties that fuel violent cross-cultural encounters. Both communities practice hospitality, though hostility is the natural expected behavior. The encounter becomes a sacramental experience!

Reading the text with this in mind helps us see how the social and cultural location of Cornelius, an outsider, gave him a privileged position to take the initiative of the encounter. Whereas Peter was tied to his cultural background and religious worldview, Cornelius was held captive to a particular notion or understanding of what God can do. God proved to Peter, through the power of the Holy Spirit, the recognition of these Gentiles as God's people. God gave to Cornelius the grace and joy of salvation and inclusion to the Christian community. Both converted!

The position of placing ourselves *on the tightrope* helps us see (1) that God pushes us into a new missional opportunity, opened to the wind of the Spirit; (2) that Christian fellowship, identity, and maturity comes from communal experience, not in ethnic isolation created by exclusive cultural claims; (3) our need to understand cross-cultural mission as an eschatological moment where God invites reconciliation; (4) that the Christian faith permeates all areas of communal life, including our encounters with people of other faiths and cultures; (5) and that the social and cultural context of the marginalized, the outsiders, provides a particular location that gives a prophetic perspective to the idolatrous powers of society.

According to an essay entitled "Evangelism in the Eighties: Witnessing to a New World Order" by the late Hispanic/Latino missiologist Orlando Costas,

> It is a fact, at a time when important sectors of mainline Christianity have become stagnant and dry, and when leading sectors of the evangelical, fundamentalist, and charismatic movements have embarked on a neo-Christendom project, and have incorporated the illusion of a Pax Americana, and an exclusivistic "American Dream," large sectors of the church of the poor and disenfranchised are bearing a vigorous witness to the gospel—without fanfare, financial resources, or academically qualified personnel. Black, Hispanic, Asian, and Native American churches and Christians, in partnership with a minority from the mainstream society which has identified itself with the poor, the powerless, and the oppressed of the land, are witnessing to the new world order announced in the gospel.[1]

Strategies and Theology for Cross-Cultural Mission in Congregations

How can we prepare our communities for cross-cultural mission, whether cross-cultural, short mission trips, cross-cultural mission in our own communities, or mission in general?

1. Christian communities need to provide a learning, caring, and affective space for mutual encounter and dialogue. Many Christian groups have taken risks when they engage in a common worship experience with people of different traditions or different faiths. However, many times issues and fears have been covered and kept secret in the context and content of the gatherings. As long as these issues and fears are not confronted and mutual risks are not acknowledged and appreciated, exclusion will continue to act as a phantom at different levels of the encounter. Therefore, leaders need to envision a context where faith and love can be shared, open to the process of the encounter itself.

2. Participating in cross-cultural mission requires mutual patience and compassion. Patience, because there will be times when our plans and objectives will not be accomplished. High expectations and ambitious, planned objectives can harm the process. People need to meet one another in their own social and cultural places; they do not need to be pushed or pulled into an agenda determined by other external factors, including cheap reconciliation and fragile interaction. Achievable, nonimpressionistic, and long-term flexible objectives should be in the minds of Christian leaders. Training in the area of cross-cultural communication is needed.

Compassion needs to be a fundamental ingredient in this missional encounter. I remember the story of one of my Korean students. In his Clinical Pastoral Education course he found himself listening to a hospitalized white woman who was bluntly expressing her concerns, confusion, fears, and ultimately her racism toward people of color, especially African Americans. He also heard this woman who was ill speak about the intrusion of foreigners and the deteriorating effect that they had on her community. In the beginning he was numbed by her words, later he was upset and disturbed, asking himself what he had to do with this sick, fear-driven woman who was surely blind—maybe by his chaplain's attire—to the fact that he was not Caucasian. He could have just walked out of the hospital room, with good reason. The student, however, listened and intentionally continued to visit this woman, not only caring for her spiritual need in her illness, but also searching for ways to help her recognize her racism and fear, and begin to guide her to repent from her racism and discover a new perspective regarding the "cultural others" who surrounded her. He did not react to racism, but rather he responded with Christian compassion—love with a prophetic edge—in order to enter the difficult process of reconciliation and the possibility of mutual growth through cross-cultural mission.

On a more personal and reflective dimension, he also discovered the multilayered dynamic of racism, and how, though not a Caucasian and aware of the history of racism against his people, he had some level of privilege given his ethnicity—closer to white than black skin color.

3. Cross-cultural mission is grounded in the Christian experience of liberation and reconciliation. Reconciliation begins with the oppressed. The invitation for reconciliation comes from those who have suffered the consequences of cultural, economic, political, and social displacement, and oppression. It is *the* fundamental prerequisite for the sharing of faith experiences and convictions without the fear of shame or embarrassment. The Christian conviction and action of reconciliation provides the certainty of heart and mind for the cultural encounter. This is especially true in the context of minority groups where the dominant culture has already established the qualifications for appropriate and accepted social standing and hierarchies.

For the dominant culture, this reconciliation process is difficult. Many of us who have been participants in the oppression of others and who have recognized our evil doings want immediate reconciliation. Our eagerness to receive forgiveness, given our guilt-driven culture, is our worst enemy in the process of cross-cultural reconciliation. Nevertheless, reconciliation slowly eradicates this "guilt" and moves us toward justice for the oppressed. Trust and mutuality slowly emerge as the groups continue to perceive, develop, and experience the sacramental bond that comes from the gift of the Spirit. Whether part of a minority group or of the dominant culture, both groups will be nourished and challenged by the discovery of the Spirit of God in the reconciling encounter.

4. Cross-cultural mission acknowledges the mutual recognition of incomplete, partial communal visions, with the understanding of the privileged location of those at the margins. Cross-cultural mission recognizes the particularity of cultures and the need to dwell in one another's cultures in order to see and develop more comprehensive communal and missional visions. Here again Acts 10 speaks eloquently when Peter's encounter with Cornelius's household confirms (a) the prophetic and corrective character of Cornelius's household in relation to the religious culture and worldview of Peter's religious experience; (b) the mutual clarification that comes from the encounter; an active participation and interpretation from both groups regarding both visions and experiences; and (c) the challenge to openness as the Spirit keeps a broad horizon where the cultural shape of the Christian faith is always nourished by the *cultural other*, especially the one that is most strange to dominant cultural practices.

5. Cross-cultural mission is a sacramental activity. The missional encounter of cultures needs to establish a roundtable for sharing food and nourishing dialogue. The Lord's Table is an important symbol for cross-cultural mission. Christ invites all of God's people to participate in the Lord's feast. This sacred space dramatically reconfigures and challenges our reality, leading us to God's reality, the Reign of God. In worship, the reign of justice, reconciliation, and peace is at hand, and we need to repent, convert, and become, as a community, a sign of God's Reign. The Lord's Table, hence, becomes a symbol of what our daily life should be: inviting the Christian community to progressively and critically engage the perspectives, visions, and experiences that emerge from our cross-cultural encounters. This is where the prophetic dimension of the gospel renews our Christian faith. The roundtable provides the theological and missional space for embracing the historical transformation from a powerful and affluent style of mission and ministry, to a humble, learning, and accompaniment-driven mission practice and agency.

6. The dialogical and programmed activities of cross-cultural mission need to be seasoned with devotional and spiritual mutuality. Coming together for worship and witnessing becomes a crucial factor in faith exchange and transformation of both communities. The sharing of a baptism, the Eucharist or Lord's Supper, singing, praying together, sharing our faith journeys, sharing our

weaknesses, and requesting prayer and support; all of these develop an affectionate communal character that informs the missional and worship day-to-day life of the people. People discover, learn, and develop spiritual intuition in the ecumenical exchange of worship.

This is a critical piece when relating to non-Christian groups in our context. This is an area that needs more exploration. However, good interreligious theology and missiology comes from the encounters themselves, not from *a priori* convictions that may be informed by stereotypes and misinformation. This is another gigantic step (and risk) for many congregations in urban and inner-city settings.

7. Finally, cross-cultural mission will occur as Christian communities offer mutual hospitality and recognize *time*, not as money, but as a gift of God to know one another. One of the most dramatic characteristics of the church in Acts is its hospitable character to fellow Christians and others in the community. It is that day-to-day experience of spending time in the Temple, breaking the bread at home, praising God, and having the goodwill for all people (Acts 2:46-47) that makes mission possible and life-giving. It is a spirituality of hospitality and time that allows the Christian community to discover and celebrate the "mystery of the Body of Christ"—that unique experience of being one and different at the same time and space. Many missiologists contend that Acts is more than the expansion and growth of the church. It is the coming together of rich and poor, of Gentile and Jew, of people of different cultures affirming a common bond that shapes and gives direction to their faith commitments in their own contexts and particularities; a common bond framed within the privileged Christian location of the poor and the most vulnerable.

Hospitality in cross-cultural mission is an invitation to accept and engage in a process of reconciliation, of dwelling in one another's reality, and knowing one another. It is an opportunity to learn how to *humanize our experience with God* in a powerless and marginal situation within the new world order. It is a prophetic call to accept the challenges of being prophetic in a society pulled by the powers of consumerism, ragged individualism, and emotional exploitation. It is an opportunity to share "that which we have seen, heard, and touched": Christ's gospel of the Reign of God.

Cross-cultural missional encounters offer a unique opportunity for mainline churches to have a hard look at their practice and theology of mission. An affluent, large congregation in North Carolina established a partnership with a small, poor congregation at the United States-Mexico border, in the town of Piedras Negras. The United States congregation had coordinated with leaders of the Piedras Negras church to build an annex to the church building. Members of the mission committee spent significant time organizing and acquiring the material for the enterprise.

The United States mission group arrived and immediately began the building project. Members of the Piedras Negras church offered a warm hospitality, sharing their homes, food, and friendship. During the two weeks of the mission project, the mission group was overwhelmed by the efforts of this small congregation to provide all the needs of the mission group. The mission group was amazed and blessed by the witness of love and care that the Piedras Negras church offered to them. The mission group had come to a consensus regarding their experience in Piedras Negras: we have received more than we have given.

Leaders of the mission group and the local church arranged a worship service to close the mission project. During the service, both congregations shared food and testimonies of new friendship, of newly discovered sisters and brothers in Christ. As the service came to its conclusion, members of the Piedras Negras church offered their homes for future mission trips: "Nuestra casa es la casa de ustedes; ustedes son de la familia" ("Our home is your home; you are part of our family"). In an act of mutual reciprocity, members of the mission group invited and offered their homes to the Piedras Negras church. It was a service of intense mutuality where the Holy Spirit brought these people together.

Accepting the previous invitation and the offered hospitality, three weeks later a group of twelve young men crossed the border and stopped at the congregation in North Carolina. The group, en route to farms in the Northeast where jobs awaited, was looking for a place to stay overnight. The mission group was excited about their visit, until it was known that all of them had crossed the border with no documentation. At this point, some of the members of the mission group and other members of the congregation requested a meeting of the leaders to examine the situation. By the end of the meeting, the leaders had decided that the twelve young men could not stay in the premises of the church building; they needed to continue their journey to the North.

The pastor of United States congregation had an acquaintance in the Hispanic/Latino Pentecostal church in the downtown area. She immediately called her friend and in less than an hour the Pentecostal congregation was offering the twelve young men the needed hospitality. Some of the members of the mission group joined the efforts of the Pentecostal church, though saddened by their leaders' decision.

A Presbyterian congregation in California opened its doors to a Hmong group. (Hmong is an ethnic group from Laos who were persecuted during the Vietnam War and became refugees of war. Many came, and still come, to the United States to reconstruct their lives.) This congregation offered all kinds of services—housing, medical and health orientation, education, legal, and many more—and they provided a space for the Hmong to nourish their spiritual needs. The Presbyterian congregation was an example of hospitality. Members of the church also expected that at some point the Hmong group would join their congregation, thus making it a more diverse church.

Progressively, the Hmong began to take control over their lives. They were appreciative of the Presbyterian congregation and expressed their gratitude with gifts and food. They, however, had established their own congregation and slowly but steadily distanced themselves from the Presbyterian congregation. It was clear for the host congregation that their Asian friends were moving in a different direction, incompatible with the vision and expectations of the Presbyterian congregation.

The pastor of this congregation was taking a course with me. He shared this story after I had spoken about the cross-cultural challenges in mission for the United States context. He was frustrated with the outcome of the project and hoped that his congregation would be enriched by the presence of the Hmong. As he continued to address the different issues in his congregation's story, I asked him the following question: "Would your congregation do it again with another ethnic/refugee group?" The pastor looked at me hard and took some time to think through his answer. With a smile on his face, he replied: "Yes, professor, our congregation would do it again. We learned so much about who we are and who the Hmong are. . . . We have never been the same, though we may not think about it too much; we have become a different congregation. We discovered a new spirituality, a missional spirituality."

As we seek to become God's missional people *walking the tightrope*, aware of the complex cross-cultural dynamics involved in mission practice and theology, I would like to suggest in the next chapter some educational resources and disciplines that can contribute to developing a *global Christian spirituality* that will guide us in our journey of faith and mission.

1. Orlando Costas, "Evangelism in the Eighties: Witnessing to a New World Order," mimeograph paper, 1981.

CHAPTER SIX

Mission and Theological/ Christian Formation

After surveying mission theologies and practices, and discussing many ideas and principles regarding mission, I am quite certain that any person who wants to do mission, be it crossing geographical boundaries or crossing economic, cultural, or social boundaries in her or his own context, needs a strong and healthy theological formation. For a long time mission societies and Christian denominations have considered *the calling, the motivation, and the willingness* of the believer or believers to be the critical defining criteria for missionary work. Today we know that these principles are not comprehensive enough. There is an urgency to prepare people and congregations for mission in this new millennium with an awareness of the historical context where mission work is to be done. Persons and congregations need a strong cross-cultural formation and a solid theological and interdisciplinary education. The power struggles, economic conflicts, religious tensions, cultural wars, and deterioration of the environment require missionaries and congregations, whether with a long- or short-term commitment, to develop what I call a *global-Christian spirituality* to discern and act faithfully for God's mission in the context where they are called to serve.

As I explained in chapters 4 and 5 (and in the diagrams in the appendix), we always encounter another culture/religion with our own cultural presuppositions and understandings. We never understand "the cultural other" on her or his own terms. Our cultural encounter is always mediated by our own cultural lenses, just as "the cultural other" understands us with her or his own cultural lenses. The *global-Christian spirituality*, however, is an attitude, an inclination, an outlook, an understanding of life, a cosmology, a practice, and a reflection of faith and life that (1) recognizes the difficult but crucial cross-cultural dynamics in any cultural encounter; (2) acknowledges the complex and multiple realities—economic, social, gender, ethnic—in a particular context, and the way in which those realities affect other contexts; (3) discerns and participates in the *missio Dei* with an awareness and critical perspective of the above dynamics; and (4) continues to grow and develop (through spiritual disciplines and cross-cultural training) in the Christian faith. *Global-Christian spirituality* is undergirded by a conviction that the understanding of the sacred is changing in the world, thus, our missiology needs to be grounded in the day-to-day experience of the people, in a Trinitarian relational mission theology, and in an eschatological expectation of the coming Reign of God.

It is evident that this *global-Christian spirituality* grows with experience, introspection, prayer, Bible study, worship, and integration. Nevertheless, it also grows as part of a strong educational and formation process. This process helps communities give perspective and grounding to missionary experience. Deep, faith-committed, visionary, and coherent theological reflection is an important ingredient of such process of formation. Missiology is the discipline that contributes to our understanding of the *praxis* of mission.

Missiology is an interdisciplinary discipline. It builds on the use of history, theology, biblical studies, anthropology, religious studies, economy, sociology, and others, including the natural sciences. The field is resourceful in the many ways in which it uses all of these disciplines. This book, for instance, attempts to use many disciplines to convey the challenges faced by Christian mission in the new millennium. The question is, however, *What disciplines can best contribute to develop the global-Christian spirituality and a Christian missiology?*

Rediscovering Old Disciplines for Mission: Theology, History, Bible, and Worship Studies

Theology needs to be rediscovered in our missiological reflection. Unfortunately, our mission practice and theologies, as described in the different mission models in chapter 1, continue to marginalize theological reflection in our mission practice. But theology still needs to develop a missiological approach. For too long theologians have reflected on the great theological themes—the Trinity, God, Jesus Christ, the church, the Holy Spirit, the sacraments, and others—with little missiological awareness and import. For too long the theological task has been an abstract reflection difficult to understand in the life and mission of many communities. Therefore, *good theology should be missional, and good missiology should be theological.*

It is imperative for our theological and educational formation to integrate the great theological themes to questions regarding our mission theologies and practices. For instance, our task to witness to people of other faiths needs to be informed and shaped by the rich theological reflection regarding the Holy Spirit. Assumptions about the participation of God in the life of people of other faiths need to be reevaluated and even changed as we struggle to understand the Christian tradition's reflection on the Holy Spirit. It is not enough, and even unacceptable, to disregard people of other faiths on the basis of the religious and cultural superiority of past centuries.

History and missiology need to find each other in a new way. For many years and for many historians, particularly in the Western Hemisphere, there has been a distinction between Christian history and mission history. Frequently, such a distinction assumes Christian history to be either a history of Christian thought, a history of a denomination, a tradition, or a congregation, usually focused on the context of Christendom. Mission history, on the other hand, is about legendary missionaries, heroic adventures in faraway lands, civilizing efforts, and denominational growth and stability in the non-Christian continents. Consequently, the reader can find books on church history and mission history, but rarely are both disciplines integrated. Probably the most eloquent example of this distinction is Kenneth Scott Latourette's two volumes, *Church History*, and the nine volume *History of the Expansion of Christianity*. Though Latourette was uncomfortable with this distinction (and contributed to reducing the gap), he wrote under its rubric, affirming such a legacy from Christendom.

History has the challenge of incorporating the dynamics found in the transmission and reception of the gospel in different contexts. On the transmission end, it has the task of helping the student of history understand the struggles, discernment, and activity involved in sharing the gospel. On the reception end, it has the task of helping the student see the complex process of the contextualization of the gospel, the multilayered process of how the gospel is rooted in a particular context. It has also the challenge of naming the challenges and keeping the coherence between the particular histories of the people of God and the universal history of the Christian community. Today we are witnessing a different approach to Christian history as many Christian historians become aware of the missiological contribution to this discipline. *Good history will not only narrate events or biographies, but will provide meaning to the story of the people of God in their task of discerning and participating in the mission of God.*

Biblical studies and missiology need to rediscover each other. Chapter 3 attempts to provide some of the conversation that has already begun between biblical scholars and missiologists. It is imperative, however, for the conversation to continue and to be broadened. *Good biblical theology and missiology nurture each other. Both disciplines, in conversation with each other, can provide lenses that will help the Christian community faithfully explore missiological issues with a sense of continuity, rootedness, critical approach, courage, and creativity in harmony with the witness of the people of God in the Scriptures.*

The last discipline that I want to identify as critical for missiology is worship studies. Mission is about discerning and participating in the activity of God in the world. The task of discerning God's missionary activity in the world is related to worship. Mission is worship to God.

Worship is a communal practice. Even in our personal devotions we are in community, whether by reading a devotional book, praying for a close friend, or singing a hymn from the great Christian tradition. Worship provides the social and institutional space—the public space—for sharing our *testimony*. Consequently, it should be the space where God is glorified, thus made known.

It is also the space where our cultural particularities are strongly affirmed, though at times unnoticed by us. We sing, read, act, pray, and relate in our own cultural terms. Thus worship is the space where the gospel is inculturated, and therefore a space to celebrate our faith in our own particularity. It is also the space where the gospel can be diluted and confused with our own interest, thus the need for a prophetic witness. Worship is the space where the Christian community is both *object of God's blessings and subject in giving glory to God's name.* It is an eschatological space where time and space collapse and God is active as well as the center of our activity. Worship studies and missiology need to engage each other in order to help develop ways by which *good worship becomes a missiological expression where God is glorified, the gospel proclaimed and inculturated, and the congregation discovers and celebrates God's initiative in all missionary activity, which leads to reconciliation and liberation.*

Discovering New Disciples for Mission: Anthropology, Religious Studies, and Economy

In one way, this subheading is misleading. The disciplines of anthropology and religious studies developed by way of early missionary work. Missionaries contributed in a significant way to ethnography, cultural and religious studies, and cultural theory. In another way, these disciplines also developed under the influence of modernity, which created a division between the social sciences—anthropology and religious studies among others—the natural sciences, ethics, and theology, which tends to isolate the disciplines from one another. Recently, these disciplines are slowly recovering from their isolation, and in particular rediscovering their place in missiology.

Anthropology and religious studies contribute tools for interpreting the context where we are engaged in missionary activity. They open windows that allow us to see and understand cultures and religions in a different way, making us progressively aware of our ignorance and prejudices that are carried from our own cultural and religious context. As these disciplines serve as a mirror of our own cultural assumptions, we become better interpreters of the new context, of the people who we serve, and of our cultural issues and the way in which the world is interconnected. We are also provided with unique ways to interpret the gospel in a different context, contributing to the contextualization of the gospel in both the mission and our own context. *In a time of acute cultural and religious awareness, anthropology and religious studies contribute to the formation of the people of God in mission as people become aware of their own*

*cultural and religious biases and become open to the wind of the Spirit as
witnessed in different cultural and religious traditions.*

Because the world is interconnected and the gospel is about justice, mission theologies and practices need contributions from economic and scientific studies. The increasing gap between rich and
poor, and the issues behind development and technology, require
missiology to move beyond the traditional disciplines of history,
Bible, and systematic theology. Moreover, as the world faces serious environmental concerns that threaten to destroy our own plan-
et, the applied sciences, such as engineering and scientific research,
become important resources for missiological reflection and
informed political and economic strategies. It is crucial, however,
for the reader to remember that these disciplines are not value free,
but rather can be sources of interpretation that can either contribute to the well-being of creation or justify the trend of indifference and exploitation toward fellow human beings and our natural
resources.

The administration and use of money has been a critical issue in
mission activity, but it has not been given the necessary attention as
a theological and reflective task. One critical aspect that shapes and
determines the asymmetry between cultures, as studied in chapters
4 and 5, is the financial situation in mission projects and partnerships. I have heard too many denominational leaders complain
about the way in which Western Christians and congregations create internal conflicts with their money-to-mission projects.
However, there is no doubt that the economic situation in Africa,
Asia, Latin America, and the Pacific requires a financial response
from more fortunate congregations and denominations, and that
the economic desperation in the many contexts of these continents
creates very difficult situations for partnerships. Yet, temporary
solutions (and even long-term solutions) are susceptible to the
complicated economic situations of the southern continents.
Consequently, if our solutions emerge out of guilt, or pity for the
poor, or uncritical passion for a mission project, or blunt ignorance
of the economic world order, or any other reason that promotes the
doing without the reflecting—particularly on the economic complexities of the mission context—we can end up doing more harm
than good. *As we coparticipate in God's missionary activity in a broken
world, the disciplines of economics and applied sciences become crucial
in order to help missionaries, mission institutions, and congregations*

develop sound and realistic programs to help alleviate the injustices of the world. The integration of missiology, economics, and applied sciences will help eliminate the naive approach of many among the people of God regarding issues of community development, health, environmental issues, and sound economic sustainability.

These interdisciplinary suggestions are innovative and difficult to implement in many Christian congregations and institutions of theological and missional formation. The academic emphasis, therefore, needs to be tempered by the reality of congregations and theological/missionary institutions. Congregations and institutions cannot escape the challenges in mission theologies and practices for this millennium. They need to be open to the best possible education and formation for mission.

As I stated above, *global-Christian spirituality* (1) recognizes the difficult but crucial cross-cultural dynamics in any cultural encounter; (2) acknowledges the complex and multiple realities—economic, social, gender, ethnic—in a particular context and the way in which those realities affect other contexts; (3) discerns and participates in the *missio Dei*, aware of and with a critical perspective of the above dynamics; and (4) continues to grow and develop (through spiritual disciplines and cross-cultural training) the Christian faith with a conviction that the understanding of the *sacred* is changing in the world. Thus our missiology needs to be grounded in the day-to-day experience of the people, in a trinitarian relational mission theology, and an eschatological expectation of the coming Reign of God. This spirituality, this outlook and lens, is required for mission in this millennium. Without a theological and Christian formation that takes into account the above suggestions, we may find ourselves maintaining models of mission that do not contribute to the ongoing activity of God in the world. God's mission therefore, though always done despite our inadequacies, will find resistance rather than acceptance.

Conclusion

Together, we have covered significant material on theologies and practices of mission. I must add, however, that this is far from the end. On the contrary, I have exposed the reader to what I consider to be the basic and critical material emerging from the discipline of missiology for our time. As you can see, the discipline is multidimensional and interdisciplinary. I can assure the reader that with this material you will be able to grapple with some of the critical issues regarding Christian mission. Nevertheless, it is only a first but important step to beginning an exploration of a very rich, diverse, and changing discipline.

Second, I also want to assure the reader that theologies and practices of mission are always in the making. In missiology, the theological reflection emerges from the doing, from the actual engagement of Christian communities in the discernment and coparticipation in the *missio Dei*. Therefore, discernment and coparticipation are the main sources of missiology.

Third, just as missiology is born out of the practices of mission, missiology is a critical source to help Christian communities be introspective, critical, and transformative in their mission practices. Consequently, mission practices and theologies are mutually dependent. A healthy, sound mission practice accompanies a healthy, sound mission theology. A spiritually healthy, sound, and critical discernment accompanies a spiritually healthy, sound, and crucial mission coparticipation. One without the other runs the risk of losing sight of the *missio Dei*.

Fourth, good, healthy, critical, and sound mission theologies and practices are never perfect. The complex dynamics of the encounter with cultures and religions; the difficult contextual situations in our world; the challenge of interpreting and translating the gospel for a particular context; the unpredictable reception/contextualization of the gospel in the multiple and varied Christian communities; the challenge to integrate our particular histories with the history of all Christian communities; and the risk-taking factor with humility that we Christians need to develop and live as we coparticipate in God's mission will always make our mission practices and theologies temporal, contingent, fragile. Yet, it is this imperfection of mission theologies and practices that offers opportunities for mission to be transformed with the guidance of the Holy Spirit.

Fifth, our mission practices and theologies are grounded in our own testimony of faith as people in community and as people of God. Who we are as Christians, as people of God in this world and as people who do not escape from the world but love the world just as God loves it, shapes our missiology. Therefore, I want to close this essential guide with a testimony, my testimony, my statement of faith in mission. This testimony is tentative, but assertive. It is tentative because God has not given the last word and God continues to be in mission, surprising my perspectives and ideas, reforming my theology and commitments, transforming my faith and convictions, and sending me to exciting places to see, hear, touch, and smell what God does in the world. It is assertive because it is my introspective reflection of God's marvelous doings in my life and in the communities where I have served. It is a testimony of God's missionary activity in my personal and communal context. As a testimony, it is intrinsically missional and it guides my missiological vocation. As a testimony, it describes the place from where I begin my mission practice and my mission theology. Knowing where I begin helps me become aware of where the Spirit of God may take me.

I am an evangelical Christian by the grace of God, not by choice. God comes to my life as an overwhelming reality encompassing all the dimensions of my life. I do not have the truth. The truth has me.

I am also a [Third World] Christian....My biography is about multiple and interpenetrated realities and identities. These realities are political, religious, social, anthropological, historical, and theological in nature. They are about struggles for justice and self-determination; about religious cross-fertilization; about class conflict; about intercultural identity; about a painful and subversive memory, a confusing present, and an uncertain future; about violent cultural encounters and multicultural coexistence; about God's presence, activity, and hope in this conflicting reality. I am an expression of the encounter of these multiple and interpenetrated realities.

My identity as an evangelical Christian, therefore, is also interpenetrated. Being an evangelical, third world Christian missiologist is about living at the border, fluctuating between truth and the realities that have me. It is about being a Christian missiologist with all the contradictions, paradoxes, uncertainties and complexities that shape the life of Christians [around the world]. It is also about searching for insights and perspectives that can help my community discern God's purpose and activity in our histories. It is also about doing, about embodying and risking and living the faith. . . . It is also [about] searching and doing. I am as I search and do; I search as I do and am; I do as I am and search. At the border I discover the following . . .

Christian mission is the recognition, participation, and proclamation by the Christian community of God's activity in the world. As an evangelical Christian, I believe and confess that the birth, life, ministry, death, and resurrection of Jesus are the critical embodiment, the critical point of reference, the vector to understand, act, and live in God's way and to coparticipate in God's activity. As an evangelical [Third World] Christian . . . I find myself, through and in the power and guidance of the Holy Spirit, discerning, grappling, struggling, and celebrating the multiple ways in which God's activity is embodied, shaped, and understood in a context different from my own. As I cross borders to a strange space, I do it with trepidation and commitment. Trepidation, because I know that God's activity antecedes and is greater than my Christian witness. Commitment, because I can only share God's activity in my life and in the life of my community. Trepidation, because I know that my faith has been communicated many times with violence and arrogance. Commitment, because I know that my faith is not about violence and arrogance, but about peace and reconciliation. Trepidation, because I know I may find new ways of believing, speaking, and confessing God. Commitment, because I know that others may find new ways of believing, speaking, and confessing God. Trepidation, because I am risking my religious identity. Commitment, because risk is natural at the border and because proclaiming and living the Christian faith is about risk. Trepidation, because I am walking on sacred ground. Commitment, because I know that the Spirit of Christ accompanies me.[1]

111

To God be the glory in our humble coparticipation in mission, and may the Holy Spirit be our teacher as we discern, in reflection and practice, our calling and doings in the name of the gospel of Jesus Christ.

---

1. "Mission at the Borders," in *Teaching Mission in a Global Context,* Patricia Lloyd-Sidle and Bonnie Sue Lewis, eds. (Louisville: Geneva Press, 2001), 37-38.

Appendix

Transmission and Reception
of the Gospel
Intercultural Mission

Cultural Lenses

Transmission of the Gospel

Reception of the Gospel

+ A s y m m e t r y −

Cultural Lenses

1. Transmission of the Gospel

1.A Gospel is always transmitted with cultural resources and lenses of the transmitter group. The transmitted gospel is a contextualized gospel.

1.B Groups have different levels of awareness about the dynamics of transmission and reception. Few are aware of the contextualized character of the gospel they transmit.

1.C Groups have different levels of awareness about the theologies and practices of transmission.

Asymmetry Factors:

A. Cultures never meet in the same plane of reference.

B. Power and configuration between cultures shapes asymmetry. Some factors that shape asymmetry are:
 1. Economy
 2. Development
 3. History
 4. Technology

2. Reception of the Gospel

2.A Transmitted gospel interacts with cultural resources of receptor group.

2.B Reception of the gospel is also known as *contextualization.*

3.C Reception of the gospel is a complex intercultural process.

Transmission of the Gospel

Diagram One (1):
Transmission of the
Gospel

+ **Asymmetry** —

Cultural Lenses

A

Regarding point 1.B:

1. Many groups assume that the gospel they transmit is a "pure gospel."

2. Many groups are entirely unaware of or disregard the asymmetry between cultures as a critical factor in the transmission of the gospel.

3. Many groups do not see a relationship between their own process of reception (contextualization) and their transmission of the gospel.

4. Groups aware of the cultural factors and lenses in the transmission of the gospel usually try to compensate and level the asymmetry.

5. The transmission of the gospel is characterized by a complex intercultural process.

Regarding point 1.C:

1. Theologies and practices of mission do not always coincide or are congruent with one another.

2. Many times, the transmission of the gospel is assumed to be a "missional activity" with no need for theological foundation.

3. Transmission, as a theological activity, needs to incorporate the best possible intellectual and practical resources available.

4. Transmission, as a practical activity, needs to be open to a critical process of theological evaluation from both the transmitters and the receptors.

1. Transmission of the Gospel

1.A Gospel is always transmitted with cultural resources and lenses of the transmitter group.

1.B Groups have different levels of awareness about the dynamics of transmission and reception.

1.C Groups have different levels of awareness about the theologies and practices of transmission.

Regarding point 1.A:

1. The gospel is always in dynamic with a culture(s) of a particular context; there is no gospel that is not incarnated in a particular context.

2. The gospel is always transmitted from one particularity to another particularity; there is no such thing as the transmission of a "pure" gospel.

Diagram Two (2):
Reception of the Gospel

Transmission of the Gospel

Cultural Lenses

Reception of the Gospel

+ A s y m m e t r y −

2. Reception of the Gospel

2.A Transmitted gospel interacts with cultural resources of receptor group.

2.B Reception of the gospel is also known as *contextualization*.

2.C Reception of the gospel is a complex intercultural process.

Regarding point 2.A:

1. Transmitted gospel and the transmitter group experience a cultural encounter/shock.

2. The gospel is always received with particular cultural lenses, never received in a vacuum.

3. The asymmetry between two cultures significantly shapes the reception of the gospel.

4. The transmitted gospel slowly interacts with the multiple cultural resources.

Regarding point 2.B:

1. *Contextualization* is the process by which the gospel grows its roots in a particular space and time.

2. *Contextualization* considers the Christian theology and history prior to its insertion in a particular space and time.

3. *Contextualization* considers the cultural and social changes, historical and contemporary, in a particular space and time.

4. *Contextualization* considers the global cultural influences transmitted through imperialism, such as technology and others.

5. *Contextualization* is done primarily by the receptor group, though at times, the transmitter group participates.

Regarding point 2.C:

1. The reception of the gospel slowly undergoes an encounter/exchange with different cultural resources of "B."

2. The reception of the gospel undergoes complex intercultural dynamics at different fronts:

   a. Transmitted gospel with receptor culture;

   b. Received gospel with different cultural, social, and religious sources of "B."

   c. Received "gospels" received with other "gospels" received early in the history of "B."

3. The process of *contextualization* creates particular understandings of the gospel that will be transmitted in a mission activity.

4. Transmission and reception of the gospel are two sides of the same coin.

Glossary

Christendom: The fusion of a political structure early in church history, the Roman Empire, with the Christian religion. Christendom, as a political structure, is also associated with territory. Therefore, Christendom is a territory where the political structures of a group of people have fused with the Christian faith.

**Eastern/
Southern Regions:** These are the geographic regions represented by Africa, the Middle East, Asia, Latin America, and Oceania. These regions are the most populated of the world, they have the highest percentage of poverty, and they represent the locations where the Christian faith experiences vitality. Although the Christian faith had its center of vitality in the western/northern regions, in the dawn of the twenty-first century Christianity is undergoing a demographic change where the vitality and growth of the faith is experienced in these regions.

**Ecumenical
Movement:** The Ecumenical Movement (EM) is primarily characterized by those denominations that are

members of the World Council of Churches (WCC). The EM, a movement of the twentieth century, is, however, more than church members of the WCC. It is also an expression of a diverse complex of theological and missional perspectives from all over the world. The EM is a direct result of the missionary movement, thus keeping mission as a central piece in its different expressions and seeking the gift of unity given by God to the church catholic.

Eschatology: In Christian theology, eschatology is the study of the end times. For the purpose of our missiological reflection, eschatology also informs a state of being for the Christian community. This state of being is characterized as living in the end times, constantly confronting the powers of evil and destruction, and coparticipating in God's mission with hope and joy. It is an intrinsic characteristic of our missional spirituality.

Four-Fifths World: Most of the world's population is located in Asia and Africa. The fourth most populated region is Latin America. These regions comprise more than 82 percent of the world's population, hence naming them the "Four-Fifths World." These are regions overwhelmed with poverty.

Hermeneutics: The art of interpretation. Hermeneutics refers to the process by which a person or a group interprets text, symbols, codes, and so forth. When referring to "missional hermeneutics," the author means the interpretation of a text with a mission or missionary perspective.

Global-Christian Spirituality: A perspective, an outlook that allows for intercultural awareness, Christian solidarity and accompaniment, and a vision of the faith and world strongly grounded on the Reign of God and a Trinitarian missiology.

Mission: The participation of the people of God in God's missionary action in the world.

Mission Agencies/Boards: Parachurch organizations that sponsor missionaries, missionary conferences, and missionary activities. These organizations, on the forefront of volunteer mission work, contributed to the development of mission theologies in the late–nineteenth and early twentieth centuries. Some examples are the London Missionary Society and the Woman's Foreign Missionary Society.

Missiology: The interdisciplinary and critical reflection about mission.

Missional: Referring to mission. That which is related to mission.

Missionary Movement: The beginning of the Missionary Movement (MM) is usually identified with the World Mission Conference at Edinburgh in 1910. In the first half of the twentieth century, the MM represented a growing interest and concern about mission practice and theology, mostly from Western denominations and mission societies. As the movement became more global, the presence and voice of Third World Christians brought changes to the movement, both in its ecumenical and evangelical expression. Today the movement is embodied in the Commission of Mission and Evangelization of the WCC, the Lausanne movement (evangelical), and some other Pentecostal missional organizations.

Missionized: Those to whom mission is directed or who have been the objects of mission.

Praxis: Refers to a process, not simply doing. It is doing with critical reflection and introspection, discovering and developing new ways of doing mission as a result of the critical evaluation of our previous mission practice and theology.

Protestant Christendom: Refers to the process by which the historic Protestant denominations of the sixteenth and seventeenth centuries fused, at different levels, with the modern Western culture of Euro-America. It also refers to the legacy of this fusion—faith and culture—to non-Western Christian communities, theologies, and practices of mission.

Southern Continents: Refers to Africa, Asia, Latin America, and the Pacific. It is another term to refer to the eastern/southern regions or to the Four-Fifths World. It also refers to locations where Christianity is growing and experiencing vitality.

Two-Thirds or Third World: Up to 1989, these phrases coined the meaning of Four-Fifths World and eastern/southern regions. When the world was divided among the capitalist, socialist, and the "Third World" (after World War II and before the fall of the Soviet Bloc), these phrases referred to a geopolitical location and its influence in doing theology/missiology.

Select Bibliography

This bibliography is an introduction to missionary readings; it is not exhaustive. There are many more books on theologies and practices of mission all over the world. This bibliography, however, brings together what I consider to be some of the most outstanding books on mission studies during the last two decades. Some of these books have been selected by the editors of the *International Bulletin of Missionary Research*—one of the most renowned missional journals in the world—as the most outstanding in mission for the years 1989–1999 (see *IBMR* of April 2000). Others are my own selection.

The bibliography has been divided into themes, such as mission and Bible, contextualization, money and mission, interreligious dialogue, and others. All of them are about the theology of mission. Nevertheless, I have created a theme, "theology of mission," where I have selected those books that are ecumenical in scope. I hope that after reading this Essential Guide the reader will be motivated to do additional reading in the discipline. This bibliography is a resource to begin the exciting journey of broadening your missional knowledge.

Mission and the Bible

Ariarajah, Wesley. *The Bible and People of Other Faiths.* Geneva: WCC Press, 1985; Maryknoll, N.Y.: Orbis, 1989.

Koenig, John. *The Feast of the World's Redemption.* Harrisburg, Pa.: Trinity Press International, 2000.

Köstenberger, Andreas. *The Missions of Jesus and the Disciples According to the Fourth Gospel.* Grand Rapids: Eerdmans, 1998.

Legrand, Lucien. *Unity and Plurality: Mission in the Bible.* Maryknoll, N.Y.: Orbis, 1990.

Saunders, Stanley, and Charles Campbell. *The Word on the Street: Performing the Scriptures in the Urban Context.* Grand Rapids: Eerdmans, 2000.

Senior, Donald, and Carroll Stuhlmueller. *The Biblical Foundations for Mission.* Maryknoll, N.Y.: Orbis, 1983.

Mission Biographies

Anderson, Gerald, ed. *Biographical Dictionary of Christian Missions.* Grand Rapids: Eerdmans, 1999.

Anderson, Gerald, Robert T. Coote, Norman Horner, and James M. Phillips, eds. *Mission Legacies: Biographical Studies of Leaders of the Modern Missionary Movement.* Maryknoll, N.Y.: Orbis, 1994.

Krummel, John W., ed. *A Biographical Dictionary of Methodist Missionaries to Japan, 1873–1993.* Tokyo: Kyo Bun Kwan, 1996. Available from Cokesbury.

Mission and Contextualization

Bevans, Stephen. *Models of Contextual Theology.* Maryknoll, N.Y.: Orbis, 1992.

Bosch, David J. *Believing in the Future: Toward a Missiology of Western Culture.* Valley Forge, Pa.: Trinity Press International, 1995.

Christensen, Thomas G. *An African Tree of Life.* Maryknoll, N.Y.: Orbis, 1990.

Guder, Darrell, ed. *Missional Church.* Grand Rapids: Eerdmans, 1998.

Hiebert, Paul G. *Anthropological Reflections on Missiological Issues.* Grand Rapids: Baker Books, 1994.

Hunsberger, George R. *Bearing the Witness of the Spirit: Lesslie Newbigin's Theology of Cultural Plurality.* Grand Rapids: Eerdmans, 1998.

Hunsberger, George R., and Craig Van Gelder. *The Church Between Gospel and Culture: The Emerging Mission in North America.* Grand Rapids: Eerdmans, 1996.

Kraft, Charles H. *Anthropology for Christian Witness.* Maryknoll, N.Y.: Orbis, 1996.

Newbigin, Lesslie. *The Gospel in a Pluralistic Society.* Grand Rapids: Eerdmans, 1989; Geneva: WCC Press, 1989.

Sanneh, Lamin. *Translating the Message.* Maryknoll, N.Y.: Orbis, 1989.

Schreiter, Robert. *Local Theology.* Maryknoll, N.Y.: Orbis, 1985.

Mission and Ecumenism

Cone, James H. *Speaking the Truth: Ecumenism, Liberation, and Black Theology.* Maryknoll, N.Y.: Orbis, 1986, 1999.

Fackre, Gabriel J. *Ecumenical Faith in Evangelical Perspective.* Grand Rapids: Eerdmans, 1993.

González, Justo L. *Out of Every Tribe and Nation: Christian Theology at the Ethnic Roundtable.* Nashville: Abingdon Press, 1992.

Raiser, Konrad. *Ecumenism in Transition.* Geneva: WCC Press, 1991.

Sawyer, Mary R. *Black Ecumenism: Implementing the Demands of Justice.* Valley Forge, Pa.: Trinity Press International, 1994.

Schreiter, Robert. *The New Catholicity.* Maryknoll, N.Y.: Orbis, 1997.

Mission and the Environment

Hallman, David G., ed. *Ecotheology.* Geneva: WCC Press, 1994; Maryknoll, N.Y.: Orbis, 1994.

Ruether, Rosemary Radford, ed. *Women Healing the Earth.* Maryknoll, N.Y.: Orbis, 1996.

Mission and Evangelism

Arias, Mortimer, and Alan Johnson. *The Great Commission: Biblical Models for Evangelism.* Nashville: Abingdon Press, 1992.

Costas, Orlando. *Liberating News: A Theology of Contextual Evangelization*. Grand Rapids: Eerdmans, 1989.

Mission and History

Carpenter, Joel, and Wilbert R. Shenk, eds. *Earthen Vessels: American Evangelicals and Foreign Missions, 1880–1980*. Grand Rapids: Eerdmans, 1990.

Dries, Angelyn. *The Missionary Movement in American Catholic History*. Maryknoll, N.Y.: Orbis, 1998.

· Rivera, Luis N. *A Violent Evangelism: The Political and Religious Conquest of the Americas*. Louisville: Westminster John Knox, 1992.

Robert, Dana L. *American Women in Mission: A Social History of Their Thought and Practice*. Macon, Ga.: Mercer University Press, 1997.

Sandoval, Moises. *On the Move: A History of the Hispanic Church in the United States*. Maryknoll, N.Y.: Orbis, 1990.

Tinker, George E. *Missionary Conquest: The Gospel and Native American Genocide*. Minneapolis: Fortress Press, 1993.

Walls, Andrew F. *The Missionary Movement in Christian History*. Maryknoll, N.Y.: Orbis, 1996.

Mission, Justice, and Liberation

Arias, Mortimer. *Announcing the Reign of God*. Philadelphia: Fortress Press, 1984.

Costas, Orlando. *Christ Outside the Gate: Mission Beyond Christendom*. Maryknoll, N.Y.: Orbis, 1982.

Driver, John, and Samuel Escobar. *Christian Mission and Social Justice*. Scottdale, Pa.: Herald Press, 1980.

Schreiter, Robert. *Reconciliation*. Maryknoll, N.Y.: Orbis, 1992.

Mission and Money

Bonk, Jonathan J. *Missions and Money: Affluence as a Western Missionary Problem*. Maryknoll, N.Y.: Orbis, 1991.

Mission and Theology of Religions/ Interreligious Dialogue

Braaten, Carl E. *No Other Gospel! Christianity Among the World's Religions.* Minneapolis: Fortress Press, 1992.

Burrows, William R., ed. *Redemption and Dialogue: Reading "Redemptoris Missio" and "Dialogue and Proclamation."* Maryknoll, N.Y.: Orbis, 1994.

D'Costa, Gavin, ed. *Christian Uniqueness Reconsidered: The Myth of a Pluralistic Theology of Religions.* Maryknoll, N.Y.: Orbis, 1990.

————. *The Meeting of Religions and the Trinity.* Maryknoll, N.Y.: Orbis, 2000.

Dupuis, Jacques. *Toward a Christian Theology of World Religious Pluralism.* Maryknoll, N.Y.: Orbis, 1997.

Hick, John, and Paul Knitter, eds. *The Myth of Christian Uniqueness.* Maryknoll, N.Y.: Orbis, 1987.

Knitter, Paul F. *One Earth, Many Religions: Multifaith Dialogue and Global Responsibility.* Maryknoll, N.Y.: Orbis, 1995.

O'Neill, Maura. *Women Speaking, Women Listening.* Maryknoll, N.Y.: Orbis, 1990.

Sharpe, Eric J. *Faith Meets Faith.* London: SCM Press, 1977.

Thangaraj, Thomas. *Relating to People of Other Religions: What Every Christian Needs to Know.* Nashville: Abingdon Press, 1997.

Thomas, M. M. *Risking Christ for Christ's Sake.* Geneva: WCC Press, 1987.

Mission and Theology

Bosch, David J. *Transforming Mission: Paradigm Shifts in Theology of Mission.* Maryknoll, N.Y.: Orbis, 1991.

Dempster, Murray, Bryon D. Klaus, and Douglas Peterson, eds. *The Globalization of Pentecostalism: A Religion Made to Travel.* Oxford and Carlisle, U.K.: Regnum & Paternoster, 1999.

Douglas, J. D., ed. *Proclaim Christ Until He Comes: Calling the Whole Church to Take the Gospel to the Whole World: Lausanne II in Manila.* Minneapolis: Worldwide Publications, 1990.

Elizondo, Virgilio. *The Future Is Mestizo: Life Where Cultures Meet.* Oak Park, Ill.: Meyer-Stone Books, 1988.

Gittins, Anthony J. *Bread for the Journey: The Mission of Transformation and the Transformation of Mission*. Maryknoll, N.Y.: Orbis, 1993.

Jenkinson, William, and Helene O'Sullivan, eds. *Trends in Mission: Toward the Third Millennium*. Maryknoll, N.Y.: Orbis, 1991.

Johnson, Elizabeth A. *She Who Is*. New York: Crossroad, 1997.

Kirk, J. Andrew. *What Is Mission? Theological Explorations*. Minneapolis: Fortress Press, 1999.

Scherer, James A., and Stephen B. Bevans, eds. *New Directions in Mission and Evangelization, Volumes 1, 2, and 3*. Maryknoll, N.Y.: Orbis, 1992, 1994, 1999, respectively.

Shenk, Wilbert R. *Changing Frontiers in Mission*. Maryknoll, N.Y.: Orbis, 1999.

Thangaraj, Thomas. *The Common Task: A Theology of Christian Mission*. Nashville: Abingdon Press, 1999.

Thomas, Norman. Classic *Texts in Mission and World Christianity*. Maryknoll, N.Y.: Orbis, 1995.

Van Engen, Charles. *Mission on the Way: Issues in Mission Theology*. Grand Rapids: Baker Books, 1996.

Verstrelen, F. J., et al. *Missiology: An Ecumenical Introduction*. Grand Rapids: Eerdmans, 1995.

Williams, Delores. *Sisters in the Wilderness*. Maryknoll, N.Y.: Orbis, 1993.

Yates, Timothy. *Christian Mission in the Twentieth Century*. Cambridge: Cambridge University Press, 1994.

Hispanic/Latino Theologians on Mission

Costas, Orlando. *Christ Outside the Gate: Mission Beyond Christendom*. Maryknoll, N.Y.: Orbis, 1982.

——. *Evangelización Contextual: Fundamentos Teológicos y Pastorales*. San José, C. R.: Ediciones SEBILA, 1986.

——. *Liberating News: A Theology of Contextual Evangelization*. Grand Rapids: Eerdmans, 1989.

Elizondo, Virgilio. *Galilean Journey: The Mexican-American Promise*. Maryknoll, N.Y.: Orbis, 1983.

——. *The Future Is Mestizo: Life Where Cultures Meet*. Oak Park, Ill.: Meyer-Stone Books, 1998.

González, Justo L. Mañana: *Christian Theology from a Hispanic Perspective.* Nashville: Abingdon Press, 1990.

———. *Out of Every Tribe and Nation: Christian Theology at the Ethnic Roundtable.* Nashville: Abingdon Press, 1992.

———. *Santa Biblia: The Bible Through Hispanic Eyes.* Nashville: Abingdon Press, 1996.

Isasi-Díaz, Ada María. *En la Lucha/In the Struggle: A Hispanic Women's Liberation Theology.* Minneapolis: Fortress Press, 1993.

Recinos, Harold. *Who Comes in the Name of the Lord? Jesus at the Margins.* Nashville: Abingdon Press, 1997.